THE GUELPH LECTURES ON LANDSCAPE DESIGN

The Guelph Lectures on Landscape Design

SIR GEOFFREY JELLICOE

University of Guelph
1983

ISBN 0-88955-016-6 (cloth)
ISBN 0-88955-018-2 (paper)

Canadian Cataloguing in Publication Data
Jellicoe, Geoffrey, 1900-
   The Guelph lectures on landscape design

Includes index.
ISBN 0-88955-016-6 (bound). — ISBN 0-88955-018-2 (pbk.)

1. Landscape architecture — Addresses, essays,
lectures. 2. Gardens — Design — Addresses, essays,
lectures. I. Title.

SB472.4.J44 1983   712   C83-098784-3

Front Cover: The sixteenth century house at Sutton Place, Guildford, Surrey.

Back Cover: Landscape plan for Sutton dated September, 1980.

TABLE OF CONTENTS

ACKNOWLEDGEMENTS

Like his colleague the architect, the landscape designer is unable to practice his art without a commission. I am indebted to all those owners who have made such practice possible for me, and in particular to those whose private gardens are illustrated in these lectures.

The gardens for Royal Lodge (planting by Russell Page) and Sandringham (planting by Sylvia Crowe) were designed for their Majesties King George VI and Queen Elizabeth. Other owners, in the order in which the landscapes appear, are as follows: Bingham's Melcombe − Lord Southborough (planting by Brenda Colvin); Mottisfont Abbey − Mrs. Gilbert Russell (planting by Russell Page − now the National Trust); Shute House − Mr. Michael and Lady Anne Tree (planting by Lady Anne Tree); Chequers − the Trustees of the Chequers Estate; St. Paul's Walden Bury − The Hon. Sir David Bowes-Lyon and Mr. Simon Bowes-Lyon; Ditchley Park − Mr. and Mrs. Ronald Tree (planting by Mrs. Tree − now the Anglo-American Foundation); Everton Park − the Rt. Hon. Francis and Mrs. Pym; Cliveden − Lord Astor (planting by Lord Astor − now the National Trust); Horsted Place − Lord and Lady Rupert Nevill (planting by Lady Rupert Nevill); Hartwell House − the Ernest Cook Trust (research by Mrs. Pat Green); Luntley Court − Mr. and Mrs. Martin Burlton.

The gardens at Sutton Place, which are in progress, are now administered by the Sutton Place Heritage Trust. The designs were commissioned in July 1980 for his personal use by Mr. Stanley Seeger. Completed within one year (September 1980 to September 1981) the drawings testify to the eclectic influence of the owner and his contribution to making the whole greater than the sum of the parts.

The execution of these works would have been impossible without help. Of those in progress I must first record Sheila Haywood RIBA who assisted with the original plan for the Hope Cement Works in 1943 and has continued, without interruption, as the company's landscape consultant. Peter Swann FLI took over and successfully surmounted the water problems of Shute House. Of Sutton Place, Clarence McDonald RIBA of Ledward and McDonald is currently translating my concept drawings into reality. Marion Thompson FLI prepared the ecological studies described in Lecture IV. Charles Funke has conjured up plants for my wife's planting plans, and June Harrison RIBA worked with Ben Nicholson on the enlargement and construction of the Wall and made the models of the various parts of the landscape.

There are too many names to record in regard to past works, but my former partner Francis Coleridge, together with assistant Fred Tuson, were concerned in many of the projects shown, including the Kennedy Memorial, Hemel Hempstead water gardens and Horsted Place. Since the end of the war all my planting proposals (unless otherwise stated) were interpreted and carried out by my wife, as has been the photography.

Finally I must thank the landscape architecture students of the University of Guelph for showing such interest in these lectures; Professor Ronald Stoltz for responding spontaneously (while driving me to Toronto and home) to the idea of publication; the University for making publication possible; and Professor Cameron Man and others concerned in its execution, no easy matter when author and publisher are some three thousand miles apart.

Included in the text are extracts from my previous books, *Studies in Landscape Design* (three volumes, Oxford University Press 1960-70) and *The Landscape of Man*, written jointly with my wife (Thames & Hudson 1975).

Geoffrey Jellicoe
London 1983.

FOREWORD

The first three of these lectures were given to the School of Landscape Architecture at the University of Guelph, Ontario, during the week 27th - 31st October 1980. The fourth was given informally to Guelph students at Sutton Place, Surrey, England, on 27th October 1981, and more fully as the JOHN R. BRACKEN lecture at the State University of Pennsylvania on 2nd April 1982. *Creative Conservation, The Subconscious in Landscape Design* and *Space/Time* were originally prepared as independent studies. *Towards a Landscape of Humanism* was added when it became clear that the works at Sutton Place (begun in the summer of 1980) were a consummation of the three previous lectures, welding the whole into a single concept: *the recognition of the mind rather than the eye as the source of landscape design.*

The argument is that the designed landscape has always been a projection of the human psyche into its natural environment. The creative powers of the subconscious have in the past consistently informed those of the conscious and it is towards their revival that these lectures are mainly directed. To understand the subconscious it is necessary to probe into instinct, with which it is synonymous.

Evolutionary instinct can be imagined as a series of transparencies placed one over another, each carrying an imprint of the experience of an era. Obviously the number of these transparencies could be infinite, but for our purpose can be separated into five categories. The first and lowest, the primeval, could be called *Rock and Water*, so remote as to be scarcely perceptible and certainly without a known influence on the psychology of the present day. Above this is the clearly visible *Forester* of the sub-tropics. Above this the *Hunter*. Above this the *Settler*. Finally comes the unfinished transparency of our own era, which might be called the *Voyager* in contrast to the *Settler*. All these transparencies form a single immensely complex pattern, the basis from which creative landscape design will spring.

* * * * * *

Most small domestic gardens to-day are inspired by the instincts of the *Forester*. This period of more than fifty million years up to the second millenium was one in which nature as a marvellous green city evolved and fashioned physical man. When, as *Homo erectus*, he finally left the forest matrix to become the hunter he took with him not only a revolutionary new form but the efficient animal machinery by which that form was serviced. This included acute sensory perception and the transmission to his mind, through the senses, of a scene that would now be termed "beautiful" but which to him was no more than an efficient self-perpetuating larder.

From this second transparency stems all that is specifically sensuous and tactile in landscape design, especially an irresistible love of flowers, still seductive to man and insect alike.

The third transparency, the *Hunter*, shows man to have been transformed from a peace-loving vegetarian into an aggressive carnivore. Over a period of some two million years we first see him moving with cunning and exhilaration across the shrubby African savannah and afterwards migrating and adapting himself to the very different climate and geography of Southern Europe. The transparency reveals that he has discovered his own identity and his superiority to the animal. He speculates upon the meaning of his existence, peering for the first time into a world beyond the visible and finding unseen gods in all things. Paradoxically, it may have been the intolerable conditions of Southern Europe that actually called forth, in the cave paintings of 30,000 years or so ago, the first landscape spatial art.

From this idealistic transparency comes much of the English eighteenth century romantic landscape: from Africa the understandable pleasure in undulating grasslands dotted with trees and from Southern Europe the inexplicable urge for the grotesque, the hazardous, the terrible and the supernatural. (The evidence of the spirit and technique of the cave paintings suggests, too, that from this now global transparency sprang the civilisation and arts of the far east, where biological man persists to this day).

The fourth transparency, the *Settler*, depicts western civilisation from about ten thousand years ago to mid-sixteenth century Europe. The era began through the discovery of geometry as a means of defining territory in an agricultural rather than a nomad economy. Through geometry came a change of gods. The biological earth gods were unreliable and unpredictable, but not so the new found gods of the heavens, for their laws appeared unchanging and absolute. Mathematics were divine, and as their interpreter on earth, man in due time saw himself also as divine. From now on his developing intellect would battle to suppress if not eliminate all that was inexplicable, mythical and fearful and replace them with the rational and the tranquil. From this fourth transparency we inherit the sense of nobility that comes from judgement, symmetry, balance and proportion in all things, including classical architecture and its sometime dependency, garden design.

*   *   *   *   *   *

We now come to the fifth transparency, our own.

The style in Italy known as Mannerism extended from the mid-sixteenth century to the mid-seventeenth century, squeezed between the High Renaissance and the Baroque. It was a period of mental unrest, not unlike our own to-day. Faith in the church had broken down, the counter Reformation was not as yet felt, and civilisation itself seemed in jeopardy. Vignola's Villa Lante might claim to be the landscape climax of the Renaissance, but simultaneously and only a few miles away, the monsters and grotesques of the Villa Orsini at Bomarzo symbolised the terrible powers that lay beneath the ordered transparency of the Settler, now ready to break forth. For the first time in western history landscape architecture was to become an art in its own right.

Mannerism, as the name implies, is the expression of the individual thoughts of the artist rather than the collective thoughts of the age, and as such tends to flourish in times of universal uncertainty. Mannerism was able to explore the individual mind, finding in its complexities a greater flexibility than was possible in architecture, still dictated by academic rules. It revealed that a garden was more than a base to the house, as the great classicist Alberti had claimed.

The centre for this dramatic break with tradition was Florence, previously the cradle of the Renaissance. Portraiture reached a high point; Buontalenti created in the grotto of the Boboli gardens probably the first evidence of surrealism, with all that it was to imply; and an unknown designer

set out on the ground round the Villa Gamberaia at Settignano an image of the human mind that not only reflected the classic conception of its nobility, but also its idiosyncrasies and mystique. It is this brief liberating period in history that seems to have been the beginning of modern psychological landscape art and has most influenced the subject of these lectures.

*   *   *   *   *   *

The progress of psycho-analysis in garden design that began almost unconsciously in Italy was soon smothered by the more spectacular art of the Baroque, a break out from finite classical space into the infinite spaces of the imagination. Baroque was unashamedly concerned with the conquest and conditioning of the mind from *without* and was not only uninterested in the individual thought but actively against it.

Inheriting the new space concept but not the academicism of the Baroque, the quest for revealing and expressing what lay *within* the mind was continued by the English empiric philosophers. Scientific psycho-analysis in landscape design seems to have begun with the publication in 1753 of Edmund Burke's *Enquiry into the Origins of the Sublime and the Beautiful*. Alexander Pope and others had established that there could be a sympathetic response in landscape to the different moods of man, but Burke was the first to attempt to explain why this should be so. He traced the emotions of the *Sublime* to self-preservation and danger and of the *Beautiful* to the pleasures of self propagation and sex. In the eighteenth century very little could be seen of what happened below the formidable Settler transparency, but to-day we can equate the sublime and the beautiful with the experience of the Hunter in mountain or savannah. Capability Brown, an acknowledged admirer of Edmund Burke, translated the savannah into landscape, but it was the painters and poets more than the landscape designers who created the Sublime, for natural English scenery has little that is awesome and startling and the opportunities in practice were restricted. A few years after Burke's publication the critics added a third element, the so-called Picturesque, whose subconscious source we can now recognise to be that of the Forester.

While these three elements — the sublime, the beautiful and the picturesque — are recognised as pillars of the English Landscape School, there was a less appreciated fourth element of time/space explored first by John Vanbrugh and afterwards by William Kent. The reasoning seems to have been that ruins or their reconstruction carry the imagination back in time and thereby add a dimension to landscape. At Castle Howard, Vanbrugh created two deliberately separated stages of time, medieval and Roman. At Rousham, Kent co-ordinated these two stages to give the feeling that medieval England is a stepping stone backwards in time to the golden age of Greek mythology.

* * * * * *

In 1877 a professor of physiology, Grant Allen, published in *Physiological Aesthetics* the first scientific study as to how the environment should be shaped exclusively for the faculties of perception. Grant Allen was a post-Darwinian and argued that to-day's perceptions were identical with those fashioned for *Homo erectus* for a specific purpose. They needed constant exercise as well as an invitation to *feel* as well as *see* an object; thus, for example, a building in its detail should have something of the intricacies of the forests with their exciting tactile qualities to captivate and interest the eye through stereoscopic vision. Although Grant Allen maintained that his analytical method would automatically produce good architecture or landscape, in reality it was no more than a brilliantly conceived basis for it — the equivalent of the unthinking modern computer.

The end of the nineteenth century pulsated with explorations into the world that lies behind the visible. The French impressionists and post-impressionists like Monet intuitively revealed that the cosmos is not static but in constant flux. German philosophers continued the intellectual enquiry begun by Burke into the reactions of the mind to aesthetics. Geoffrey Scott's *The Architecture of Humanism,* published in 1914 was a landmark in investigation initiated by an architect devoted to the re-establishment of classical values in a disintegrating world. There followed the impact of the unimaginable world of space/time revealed by Einstein, Picasso and the American philosopher, John Dewey — the last of whom theorised that art was a continuum in which the creative process itself was the art and not the completion of it (if indeed completion were ever possible). How does the expanding and now disorganised human psyche respond to these novel ideas of existence? Can landscape design help by filling the increasing void between psyche and environment? The argument, presented empirically and only suggestively, is that it can.

* * * * * *

LECTURE I: **Creative Conservation**

The domestic garden, the nursery of modern collective landscape design, presents perhaps the most complex of all pure abstract studies in the visual arts when it is to be fitted into an historic context. The preservation of the values of history is essential, and the new proposals will form only part of a continuing process whose future is unforeseeable. The examples in this lecture, placed in a time sequence from medieval to Edwardian England, show how ethos of place differs during the centuries, and how ethos of present person differs from one individual to another. No two combinations of ethos are, nor can ever be identical, and when the designer mixes any two into a salad of his own taste, he adds a third — his own.

LECTURE II: **The Creative Subconscious in Landscape Design**

The thesis here is that in art there are two worlds, the visible and the invisible. Although the geography of these two worlds need not necessarily coincide, in practice an abstract or subconscious idea can create the visible design down to the smallest detail. Is it therefore possible to implant within a picture, consciously as well as subconsciously, an idea, that is in fact invisible but more potent and lasting than the picture itself? Two approaches are discussed: analogy and allegory, both inspired by the sister arts. A third, the most comprehensive, can be described as analytical psychology and is discussed in Lecture IV.

LECTURE III: **Space/Time in Landscape Design**

The previous lectures have been concerned with the relation of our psyche to the tangible world about us. Until the present century there was no thought but that time and space were separate and absolute in their own right. The symbol of time was the unchanging and unchangeable rhythm of day and night, the seasons and the years; that of space was Euclidean geometry. This lecture is a study of how the academic way of thought in landscape design of some fifty years ago is endeavouring to adapt itself to something never previously conceived in the world's civilised history. The lecture begins with a secure domestic scene and leads on through rational ideas to the most dramatic of all mankind's problems which he has himself created. Will he lose his identity in this gigantic supra-human world into which he has flung himself?

LECTURE IV: **Towards a Landscape of Humanism**

This is primarily a statement of classical values. If we liken our present civilisation to a ship voyaging in uncharted, dangerous seas, with no knowledge of where we are going and indeed why − then its structure is critical. Our present ship is built of the tested materials of classicism, and these we should be unwise to discard until we are certain that those of a new structure are stronger and more appropriate. But this does not apply to the contents of the ship, and as furnishings we can dredge things out of the deep that we had never even dreamed existed.

Note from the opening paragraph of David Hockney's *DAVID HOCKNEY*.*

"It is very good advice to believe only what an artist does, rather than what he says about his work. Any respectable art historian would never go only by an artist's words; he would look for evidence of them in his work. I think it was Sickert who said somewhere "never believe what an artist says, only what he does"; then he proceeded to write a book. After an artist has done the work, its reasonably easy to theorize about it, but to theorize about it beforehand could be disastrous. I don't think one should do it even if one has the inclination.

People interested in painting might be fascinated by an artist's statements about his work, but I don't think one can rely on that alone to learn about an artist's work, which is all trial and error".

*(Thames & Hudson 1976)

LECTURE I

CREATIVE CONSERVATION

Introduction

Between the Middle Ages and the early twentieth century the history of gardens and landscape in England is one of continuous change. After leaving the security of castle or monastery and venturing outwards, gardens began as walled rooms without ceilings, as at Bingham's Melcombe. The pure English pleasure garden reached its zenith under the Elizabethans and Jacobeans, the wild garden being added to the formal. Then came overwhelming foreign influence, culminating at the end of the seventeenth century in vast lay-outs laid stiffly on the soft countryside. This classical yoke was thrown off abruptly in the eighteenth century, its place being taken by the indigenous romantic English School, a landscape art independent of architecture. There was a happy confusion of styles in the nineteenth and early twentieth centuries, drawn from the past by other countries as well as Britain, and generally termed "neo".

This rich domestic heritage can be preserved in two ways: either frozen as a national masterpiece of a fixed point or points in time, or conceived as a continuum. This lecture is based on the idea that however static the architecture of an historic house or mansion may be, the gardens in which it is set can respond to changes, not only those normal and predictable in nature, but those less predictable that arise from a present owner. The resolution of the ethos of past history with that of present owner is perhaps the most interesting and compelling challenge in garden design.

The creation of a new garden in an old setting is not unlike the painting of a portrait on and within a canvas and frame that already exist. Sometimes the frame can be such as to dominate the painting; at others it may scarcely exist. At all times, however, it is the sitter and his/her unspoken feelings that are paramount, and these the artist will endeavour to penetrate, understand, portray and integrate with the setting. In landscape he will discover that in general the love of intricacies, enclosed places and flowers is a feminine instinct traceable back through the Picturesque and the mediaeval ladies' garden to the original forests; and the love of open spaces and grandeur is the male instinct traceable back through Capability Brown to the hunting savannahs. Apart from generalisations such as this there seems no rational clue to the origins in each individual of those mysterious, incomprehensible yearnings whose recognition is in fact essential to the making of an original landscape.

The thesis of this lecture is that as a study primarily in individual psychology transferred to landscape it is the first step, but only the first step, towards an understanding of the collective subconscious from which the great public landscapes of the future will emerge.

The walled gardens and dovecot.
The box parterre is a reconstruction
and the infilling by Brenda Colvin, is
a modern interpretation of use.

Bingham's Melcombe – DORSET

Supervision: 1949-79

The site for this historic but little known manor was determined by river, protective hills and agriculture. To-day it is still remote in the countryside. The earliest date of the buildings is unknown, but sometime, in the late middle ages, two enclosed wall gardens were made as open air rooms, extending from the great hall. These may have been known as the ladies' garden and the first plants may have been medicinal. The gardens were secretive and protected from a hostile environment, as it was then considered to be. Times changed, the environment was found after all to be friendly and inviting and when a Jacobean front was added to the west, the architecture was extended into a great grass bowling green that leads the eye into the distance. The age of reasoning had arrived, but not the foreign influences that were soon to become fashionable. Bingham's Melcombe is therefore an example of pure English landscape art, so well proportioned in fact as well as idea that the ethos of place resisted any change except in detail, or where additions did not impinge on the historic composition.

It is perhaps the oldest garden example in England of a balance between open and closed, surely the eternal issue in the history of landscape design – an issue deriving from savannah and forest of pre-history.

The bowling green with 400 years old yew hedge extending across the terrace walk.

*Ernest Benn, 1927

The gardens in 1926 (from *Gardens and Design* Shepherd and Jellicoe*).

View of dovecot and house with the great porch.

Luntley Court – HEREFORDSHIRE

Commission: 1982

Although the splendid entrance porch is dated 1647, this complex of manor/ farmhouse seems to be of much earlier date. The style of architecture is medieval and traditional to the remote countryside in which it is set; there is no hint of the Renaissance that began in the sixteenth century. It has always been in the ownership of one family, who today are converting it for a life style very different from its past. Originally a secluded black-and-white composition of outbuildings in the deep landscape, the dovecot was severed by a public road in the nineteenth century and the farm buildings and yard gradually allowed to decay. The proposal is to conserve the exteriors of the buildings and create from the existing conditions a new landscape that would incorporate modern needs. These needs extend from an approach drive and ample forecourt to an archery range (based on the bow and arrow used at Agincourt); from swimming pool to tennis court; from combined flower/kitchen gardens to greenhouses and arbours; and other pleasantries.

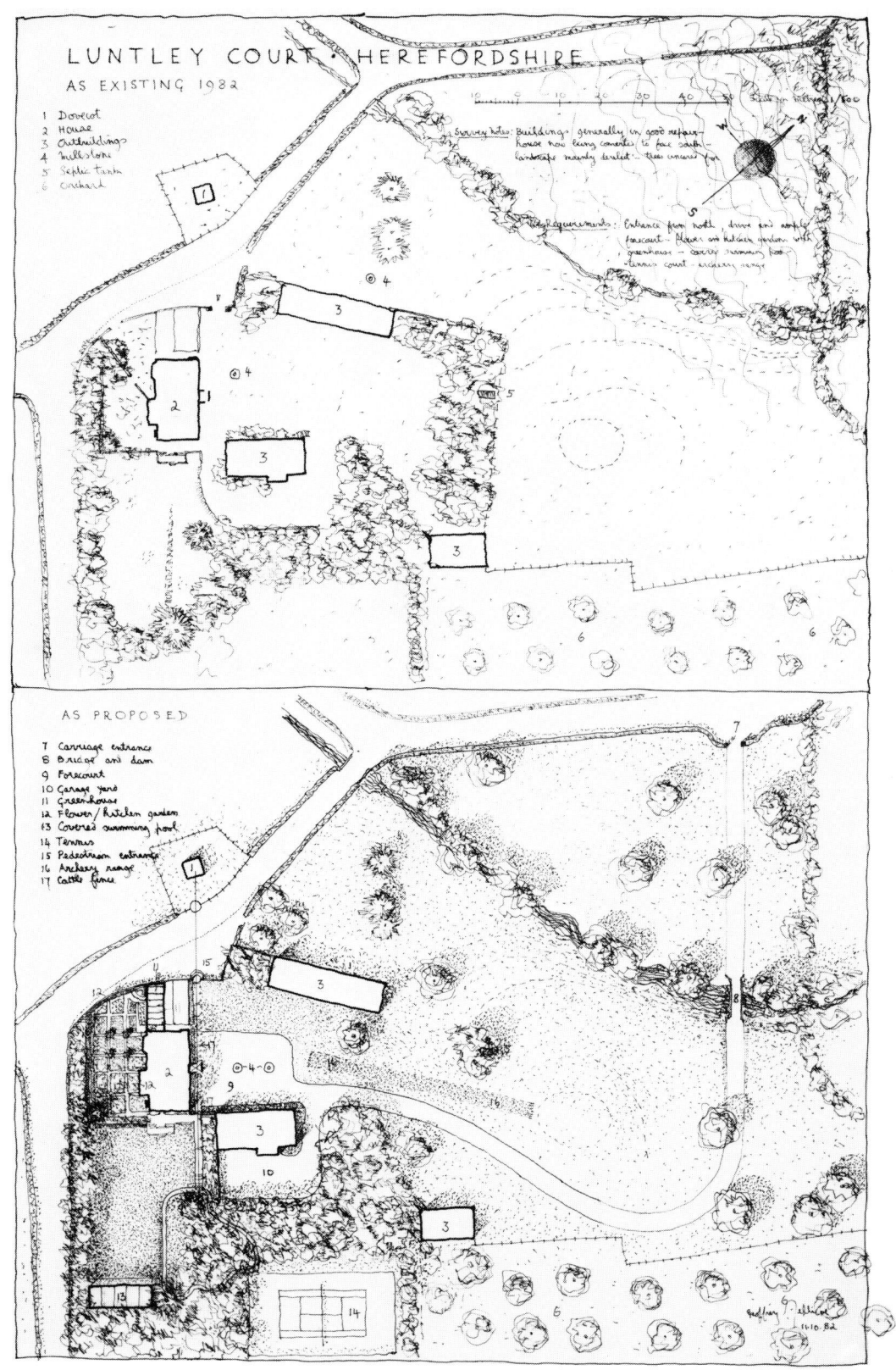

As existing and as proposed. The cattle fence in the proposals is shown returned to a traditional position close to the house, to allow sheep to come to the door. This engaging idea was impractical and has been changed to a ha-ha east of the forecourt.

Plan of 1937 – 38 from notes made in 1982.

Mottisfont Abbey – HAMPSHIRE

Commission: 1936 - 39

The Priority of Holy Trinity at Mottisfont was founded in 1201 beside the river Test in a well watered valley, sheltered from what was a bleak countryside.

It reached its climax in the middle of the fourteenth century, when two gardens were recorded. Then came the Black Death and gradual decline until its dissolution in 1536. In exchange for the villages of Chelsea and Paddington, it was granted as a private mansion to Lord Sandys of the Vine, a statesman of Henry VIII who was present at the Field of the Cloth of Gold. The approach of Sandys to his new home can be contrasted with that

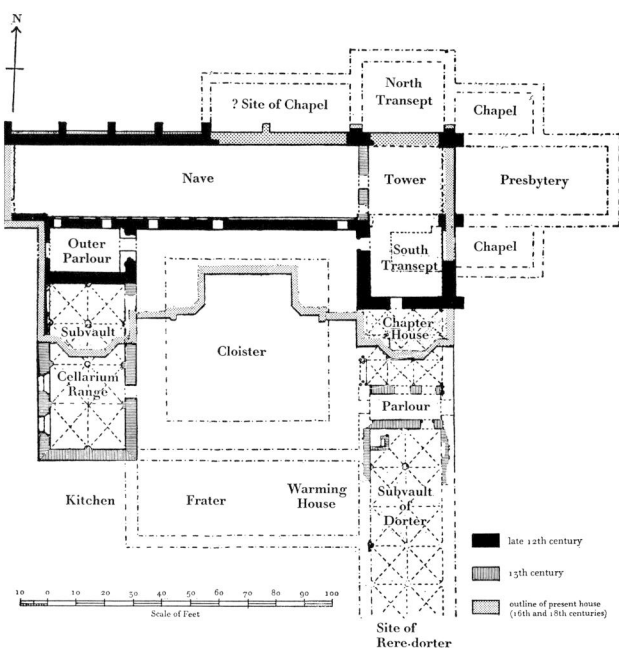

Reconstruction of the original Priory (from the booklet of the National Trust, who now own the property).

6

The pleached lime terrace and north facade.

of his contemporary, Sir Richard Weston at Sutton Place (Lecture IV). Weston was an extrovert, Sandys an introvert who adapted the Priory buildings to his needs by truncating the tower, creating a "piano nobile" within the nave (with cellars below) and demolishing the various monastic precincts.

Alterations and additions to the south front were made in the 18th century, but when the property was acquired by Mr. and Mrs. Gilbert Russell in 1934, the north and east facades – despite the windows – remained predominantly medievel. The whole was set beautifully in an English romantic style, whose trees include the largest plane in England.

In terms of art history, with lawns sweeping up to the cellared basement, the picturesque scene was complete. In terms of present day living, however, it lacked a flower garden close to the principal rooms. In addition, the early nineteenth century stables were too close to the north facade. The design that evolved was linear, muted to leave the existing ethos of place undisturbed and clearly influenced by Bingham's Melcombe. The only access to the paved walk, from the south front, began with a sunny box parterre on the site of the cloister. This path then hugged the building until it entered the terrace of pleached limes. Continuously beside the walk were shade-loving herbaceous plants.

Shute House – DONHEAD ST. MARY, WILTSHIRE

View from the west
with Donhead St. Mary in the
middle distance.

Commission: 1970-80

The present owners acquired the property in 1972, drawn as much by the landscape as by the architecture; the potential of the mixture of grandeur of setting and mystery of the existing gardens was irresistible. The estate, approached through devious lanes, lies in that area of the west country which might well be considered a cradle of the English romantic school. Wardour Castle is in sight; Stourhead and Beckford's Fonthill are neighbours; Longleat is a short way to the north. All lie in the soft landscape of rolling hills, woodlands, streamlets and villages that inspired this eighteenth century revolution against classical and foreign domination.

Panorama looking south from the house, cleared of obstruction in 1980. In the distance are the downs along which runs the ancient Icknield Way on its journey from Devon to Norfolk. Both foreground views are medieval (or earlier) fish ponds, linked by a public footpath. The shape of that to the left of the view (above) will be unaltered, but that on the right is being remodelled to link the open water with the woodlands.

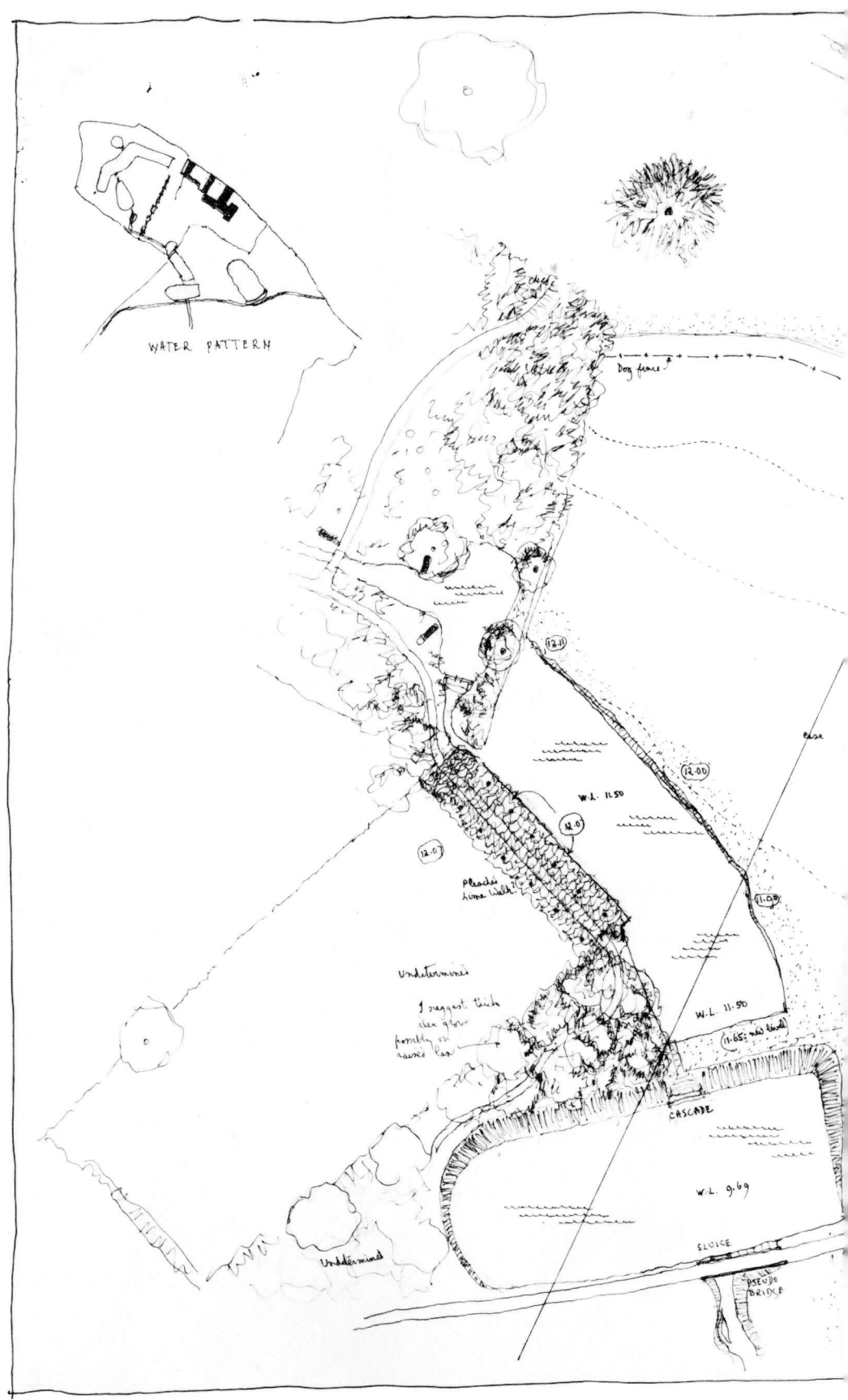

The landscape plan south of the house. The composition of light-reflecting pools is intended to create a "duality" which allows the eye to pass decisively to the far distance.

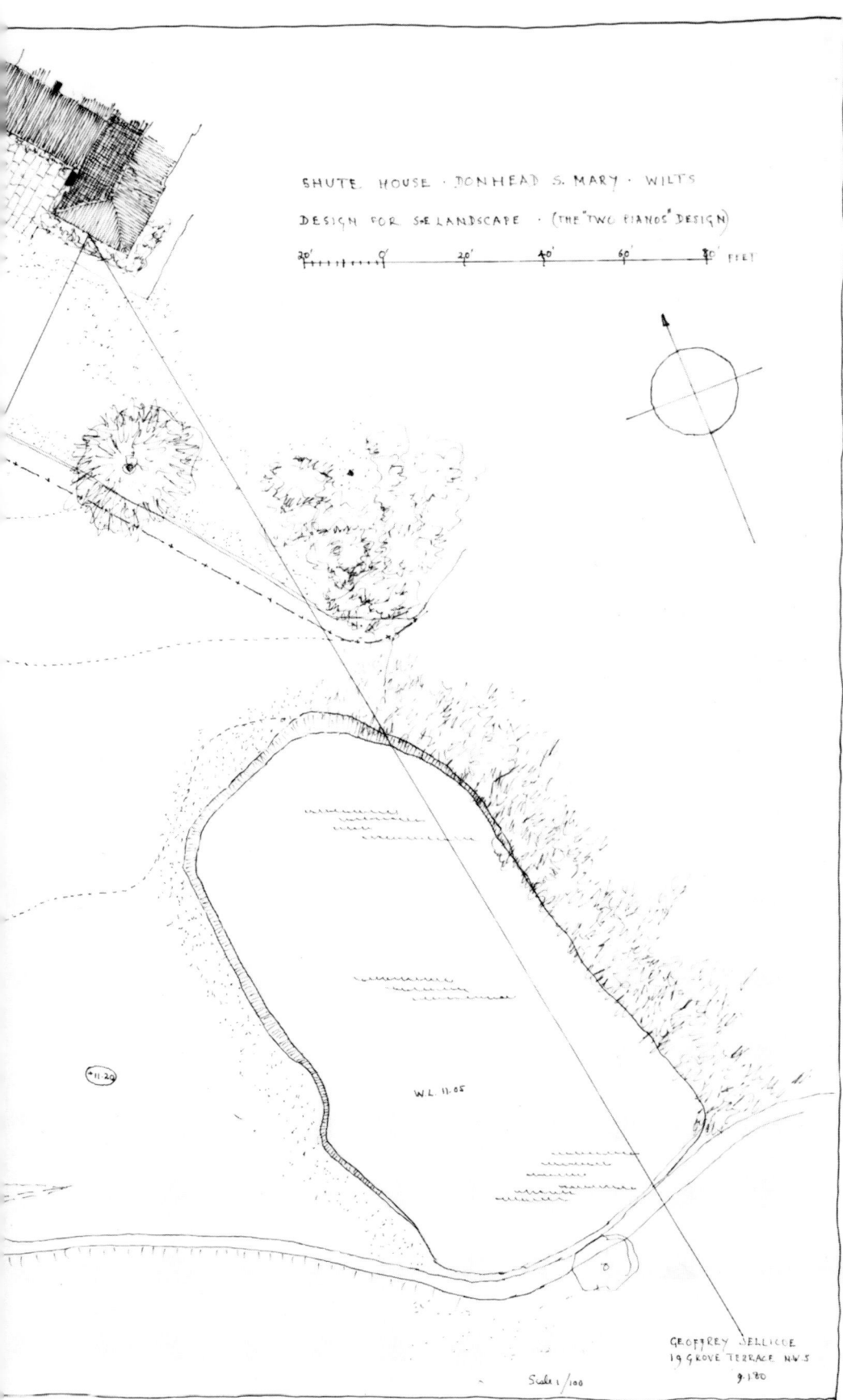

SHUTE HOUSE · DONHEAD S. MARY · WILTS
DESIGN FOR S.E LANDSCAPE · (THE "TWO PIANOS" DESIGN)

20' | 0' | 20' | 40' | 60' | 80' FEET

W.L. 11·05

GEOFFREY JELLICOE
19 GROVE TERRACE N.W.5
9.1·80

Scale 1/100

The design is known as "the Two Pianos" since the odd relationship of the pools one to another was suggested by two pianos played independently and yet in harmony.

The south elevation

The house lies directly on the south side of a lane that follows a ridge leading out of Donhead St. Mary. The front facing the village is eighteenth century Palladian; behind are buildings dating from the Middle Ages, when it is known to have been a pilgrims' rest. The site seems to have been occupied since Roman times, the attraction then as now being a perpetually flowing spring at the highest level, providing the head waters of two streams either side of the ridge. From the grass terrace before the house are seen, clockwise: a framed view of the church tower, the grand south panorama, and a curious brick wall at an odd angle. It is what lies behind the wall that has placed this garden so early in the saga of history.

The apple porch

This is the entrance to woodland gardens that are small and compartmented in space, but eclectic in time. With water, foliage and trees as building materials, the mind is invited to experience the complexities of classicism and romanticism, finding satisfaction in the unity of these two seeming opposites and traditional antagonists.

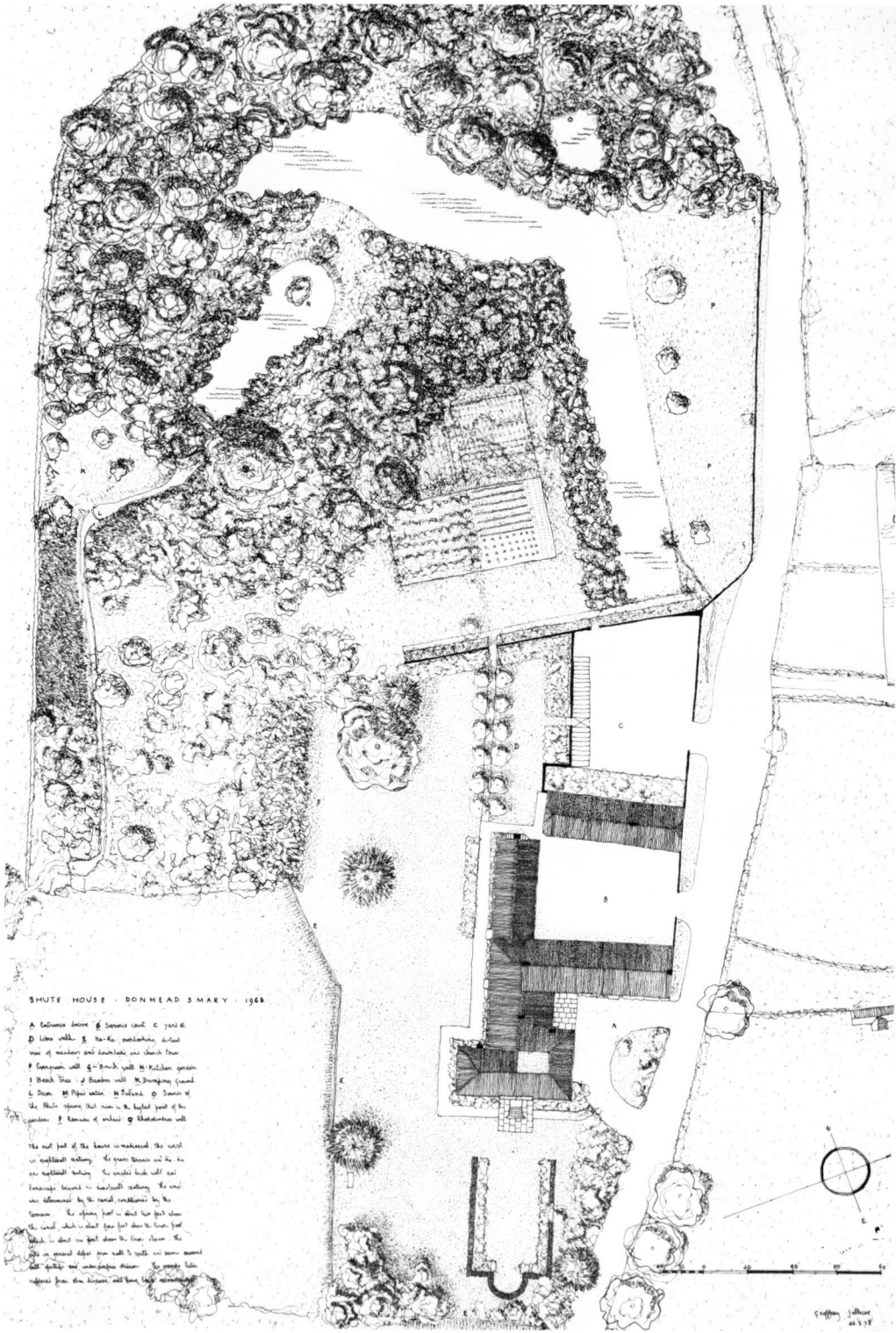

The gardens as existing before alterations. The woodlands were largely impenetrable. Many of the trees died through elm disease during progress of works.

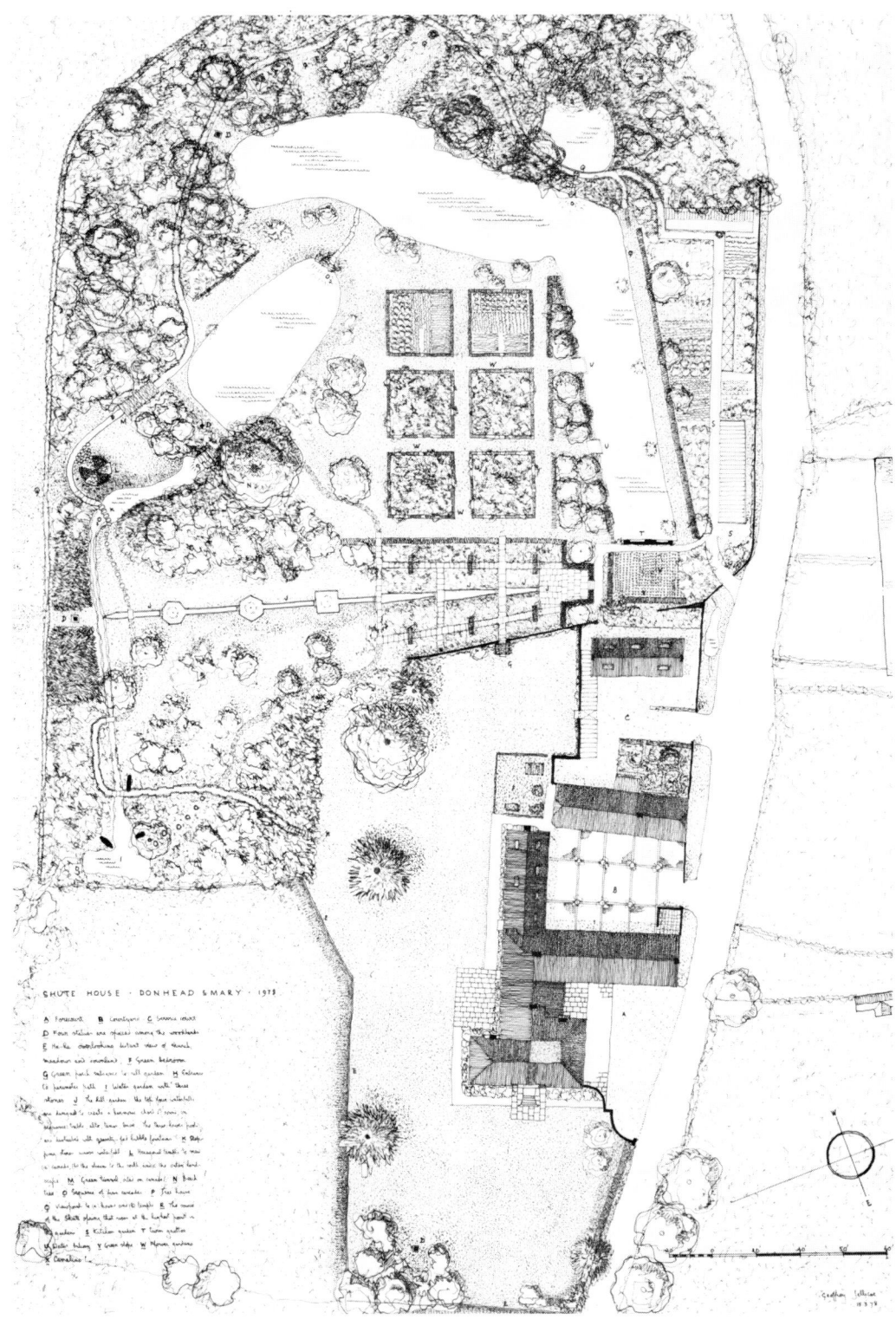

Gardens as re-designed and executed 1970-80. In principle, the house projects itself through the patterned flower beds into a world that is wholly one of the imagination.

15

The rill — looking south

There is water in abundance, embarrassingly so when it emerges from countless subterranean streamlets, but nevertheless, the cause of abnormal fertility. The sound of water is everywhere, intensified altogether by eleven small falls or cascades. The first four of eight chutes of the rill itself are designed to form harmonic chord of treble, alto, tenor, bass; but whether such an idea is unique is debatable, for any water sound would be pleasing in such a setting. In the distance is a sculpture, brought from Mereworth Castle, in Kent, the previous home of the owners.

The rill − looking north

The bubble fountains in the foreground are gravity worked, an idea derived from Kashmir. Behind the small view terrace at the summit of the cascades there was planned a conservatory inspired by that which once existed at Chatsworth, having an interior of moss or fern walls kept continuously damp. The realisation of this would have proved too costly in structure and maintenance, and its place as crucial to the composition has been taken by clipped yew and beech hedges, now high enough to disengage the rill gardens from the contrasting world of the grottos.

The grottos

The silhouette of the twin grottos brings the sequence of red-tiled roofs down to the water. The grottos illustrate an element essential to landscape art. With their black background giving an illusion of depth, they symbolise the divided flow of water either side of the hill. Our intellect knows that in fact the water itself leaves the canal ignominiously through concealed man-holes, but our imagination lifts the *idea* of the flow of water into the heroic. The grottos themselves, influenced by William Kent, are the first backward step in time as we proceed along the perimeter path.

The canal

Anti-clockwise the perimeter path leads through clipped hedges to the straight canal. In the distance is the cascade from the hidden pool, the source of the water. The path passes behind the grottos and along the canal, giving glimpses of the inner garden through the water balconies. The canal turns and the scene changes from the classical to the romantic, another sculpture from Mereworth being seen beyond the water against dark trees and foliage. The path plunges into the woodlands and arrives at the two-way seat of contemplation, one part looking outwards towards the house and the other inwards to what the Greeks would undoubtedly have designated the "sacred" spring.

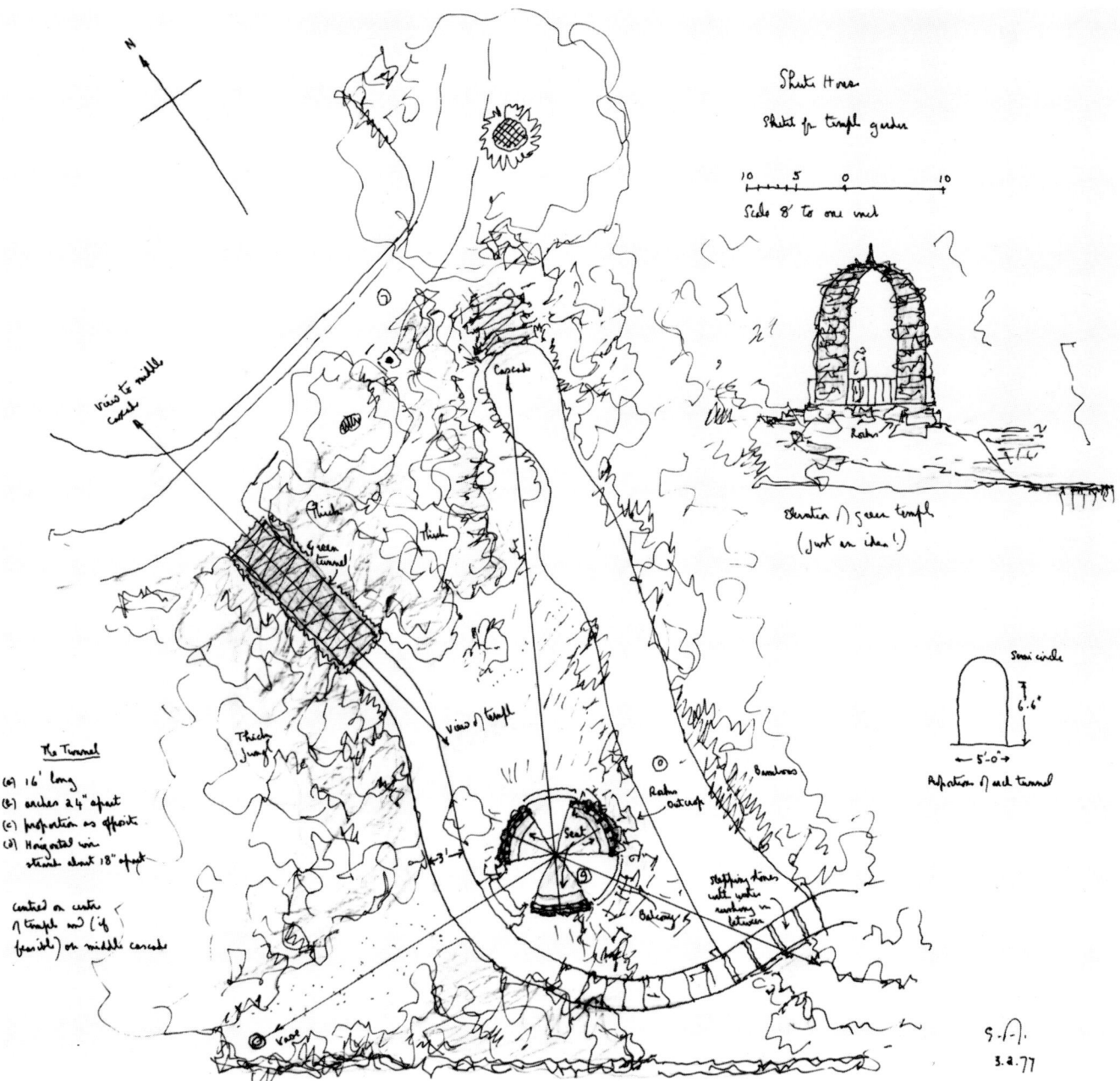

The temple

The path continues through woodlands with two accidental glimpses of the garden across water. You emerge beside a lower lake and plunge immediately into a green tunnel. Beyond, in a small exclusive enclave in the woods and open to the agricultural landscape beyond, is a hexagonal ivy temple.

This is the second step backward in time. One balcony overlooks the dark recesses of the largest of the cascades and the rivulet below, another looks towards the outer landscape, and the third (in due course) to the present-day equivalent of a mythological urn. You leave this temple by hazardous stepping stones across a lower cascade — hazardous because no eclectic landscape can be complete without an element of peril, real or imaginary.

The stone-bog garden

After threading your way through foliage and crossing the lower end of the rill, you enter the bog garden in which three great stones are set. The long journey in time ends with one of the oldest ideas in the relation of man to environment – the Chinese philosophy of an analogy between man and the rock from which he emerged, and the human significance of the stone itself. Three stones were chosen for their personality from a near-by disused quarry, and after discussion, were disposed on the site in a relationship that was unaccountably agreeable.

The "alto" cascade: a note on detail

It is theoretically possible to create a true harmonic water chord from four cascades, but scientifically speaking it will require as much research as any musical instrument. The Shute cascades are a happy affair of hit or miss, made simply of copper Vs set in concrete. The greater the number of Vs, the more fragmented is the water and therefore the lighter the tone as it falls on the calm water below. This at least is the reasoning, the Vs growing less in number as they move downstream through trebles, altos, tenors and bass.

The stepped cascade in detail

The water from its source in the highest pool finds its way southwards by two routes, one classical (canal and rill) and the other romantic (lower pool and temple) the two re-uniting before entering the bog garden. The three cascades of the romantic route are formed from stones selected from the adjoining quarry. The stones of the upper cascade were chosen for their horizontality and the specification for positioning was so simple that they were constructed by a local stonemason with an instinctive understanding of what was required.

The symmetrical N.E. elevation.

Sutton Place

Commission: 1980

The new works are described in Lecture IV. The house, built as a single entity soon after 1523 by Sir Richard Weston, a statesman of Henry VIII, is the most complete example in England of the transitional style of architecture between the medieval and the renaissance. Weston had visited the chateaux of the Loire and had been present at the Field of the Cloth of Gold.

The long south east walk with newly planted limes to be pleached.

New ideas in landscape were less advanced than those of architecture. The mansion was set in a hunting park crossed by the traditional grand avenue approach, but except for vast walled kitchen gardens, does not appear to have had the pleasure gardens considered so essential by the Elizabethans as an extension of architecture.

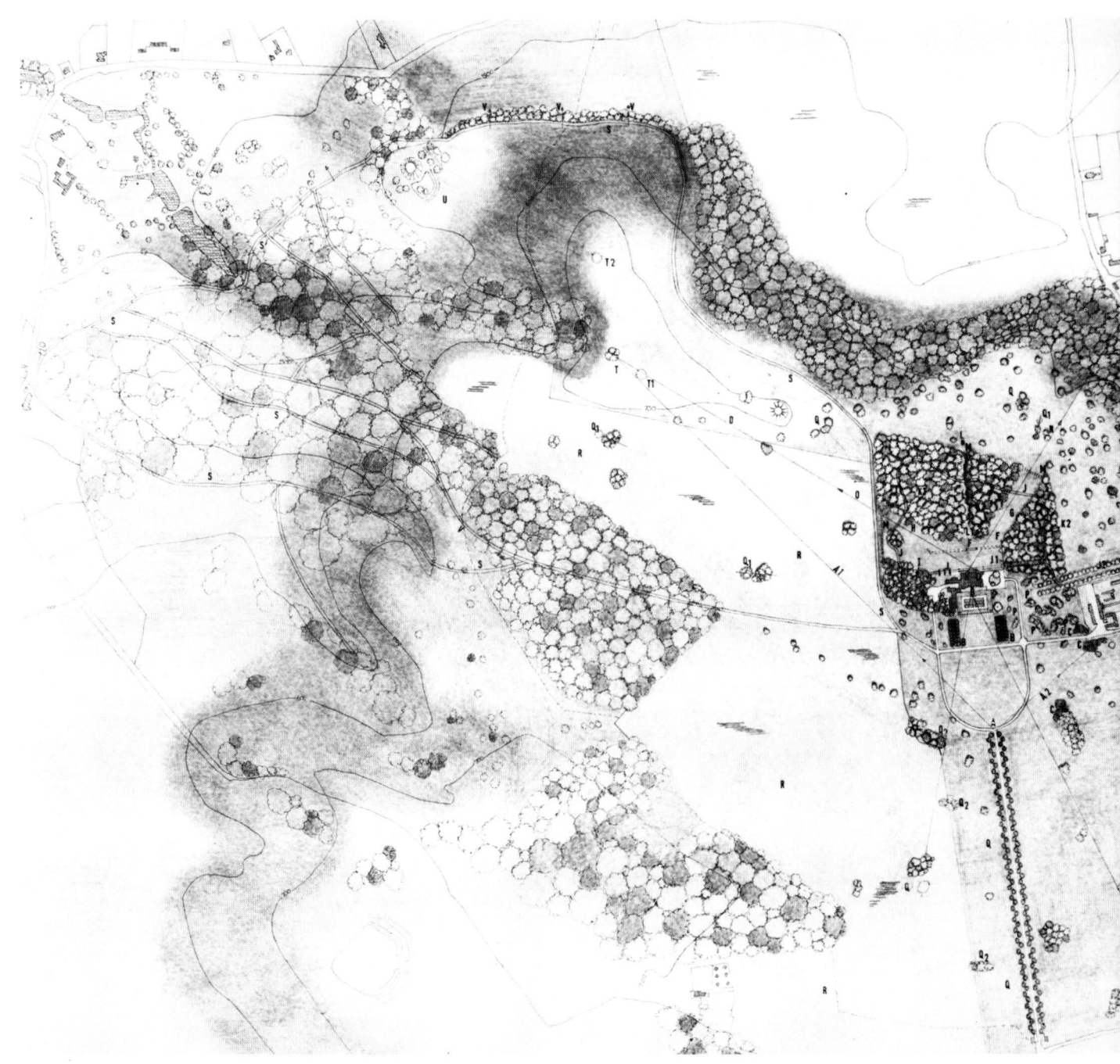

Chequers

Commission: 1972-1980

The grand concept of landscape design as a tranquilliser and restorative in an overburdened modern world was formally recognised when Chequers was presented to the nation by Lord Lee of Fareham as a country residence for the prime minister of the time – a place far from Whitehall to which diplomats of all nationalities could be invited for conference and where the Cabinet itself could meet in peace. The house itself is basically Elizabethan and additions,

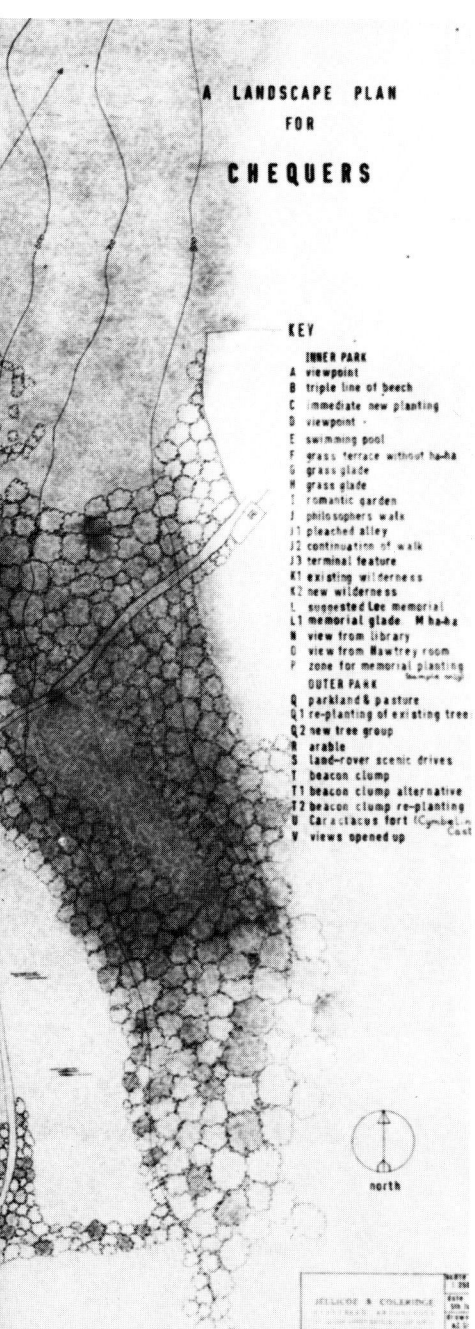

A LANDSCAPE PLAN
FOR
CHEQUERS

KEY

INNER PARK
A viewpoint
B triple line of beech
C immediate new planting
D viewpoint
E swimming pool
F grass terrace without ha-ha
G grass glade
H grass glade
I romantic garden
J philosophers walk
J1 pleached alley
J2 continuation of walk
J3 terminal feature
K1 existing wilderness
K2 new wilderness
L suggested Lee memorial
L1 memorial glade M ha-ha
N view from library
O view from Hawtrey room
P zone for memorial planting

OUTER PARK
Q parkland & pasture
Q1 re-planting of existing tree
Q2 new tree group
R arable
S land-rover scenic drives
T beacon clump
T1 beacon clump alternative
T2 beacon clump re-planting
U Caractacus fort (Cymbeline)
V views opened up

north

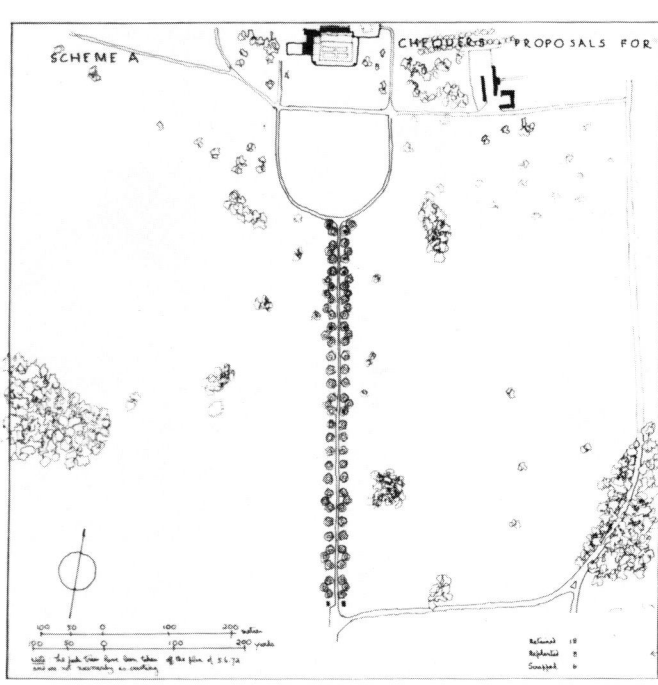

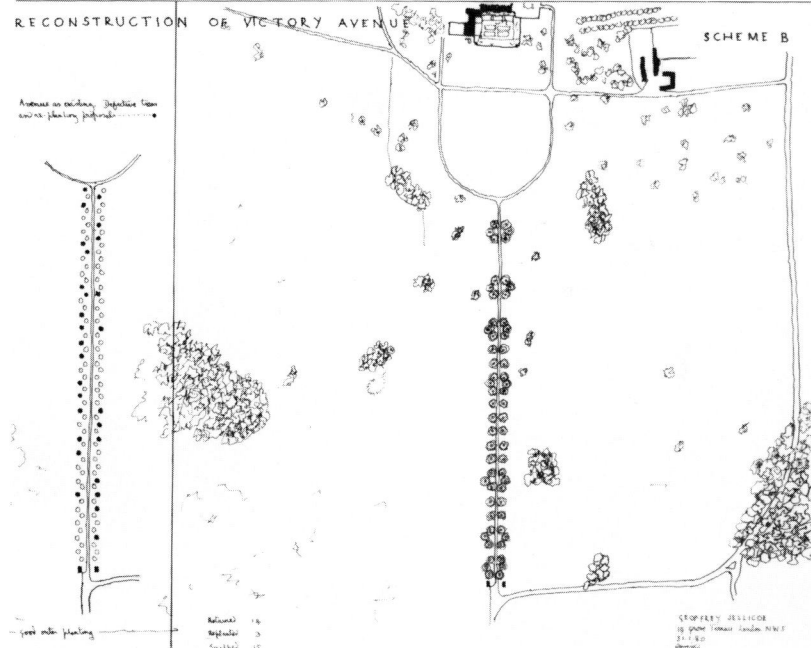

The re-design of the Churchill avenue following a disastrous attack by the grey squirrel, 1980. On the left the existing semi-mature double avenue with dead trees in black. *Above* alternative re-groupings of existing live trees. The lower was accepted since it opened up views of the landscape in which the mansion is set.

like the rose garden of 1905 and the post-war Churchill avenue, are subordinated to this style. The accompanying plan for this whole estate, made in 1972, separates the geometrical man-made inner landscape from the romantic landscape of the Chilterns in which it is set — symbolising man's endeavours to create his own ordered, stable world in one that is in constant flux and beyond human comprehension.

St. Paul's Walden Bury

HERTFORDSHIRE

Commission: 1936-82

By the early seventeenth century Italian influence was being expressed in England in the formal geometry of architecture and the philosophy that the garden was a podium of, or extension to, the house. As the century proceeded Italian influence gave way to that of France, where Le Nôtre had changed the concept of space design from one in which the garden had been subsidiary to the house to one where it was to predominate. The Court of "Le Roi Soleil" Louis XIV dictated European fashion in all things. Probably the most complete existing English domestic lay-out in the manner of Le Nôtre is St. Paul's Walden Bury in Hertfordshire, made about the turn of the century. What is lost in monumentality and a naive design technique is compensated by a domestic charm that seems inherent in all English town and country planning. It can be detected from the plan that the original north front on which the lay-out centres is unusually small in scale. With its end pavilions it seems in fact to be almost a very large "garden pavilion" in itself. When the gardens began to be restored before the last war an objective was not only to renovate what already existed, but to add others – pavilion, temples, sculptures – to terminate the vistas and to some extent recreate the flavour of the original relationship of house to richly humanised park. The structure of a Le Nôtre landscape, deriving from French hunting parks, is pure geometry, diverging only from the exact, when, like a spider's web, it must hitch on to an environment. The present endeavour is to reconstruct the web that had been mauled in the nineteenth century.

The Victorians had rebuilt the main bulk of the house and in so doing had cut away the great avenue approach from the east to open up an angle view of the new lake, purposely ignoring any centreing on the new facade. The 1978 planting is intended (a) to retain the angle view, but only as a subsidiary interest and (b) to focus the avenue on the octagonal corner pavilion by an imperceptible turn in the centre line of the avenue, concealed by illusion and (c) to prolong one of the existing avenues to cross the main avenue. The web is thus almost mended.

"Sculpture, temple and grand modelling are original. The stairway is new and intended to be a decisive introduction to a space no longer enriched with garden furnishings."

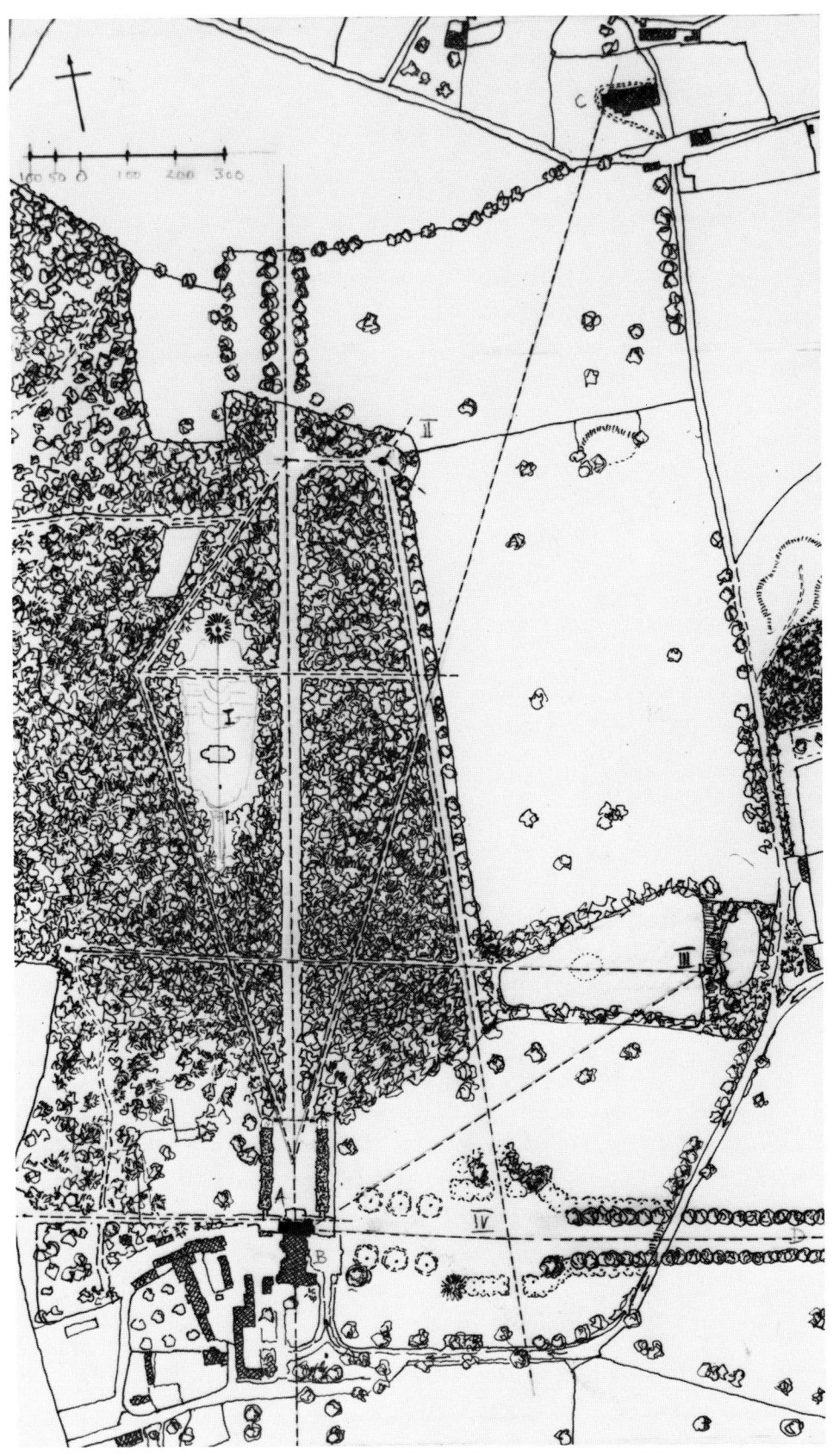

Plan showing reconstructed "web" (IV on plan). The photograph illustrates the woodland garden marked I on plan.

Ditchley Park.

Ditchley Park – OXFORDSHIRE   **Commission: 1935-39**

and

Hartwell House – BUCKINGHAMSHIRE   **Commission: 1979**

A detailed comparison of the significance of these two great houses is made in Lecture III. Both were involved in the revolution in landscape known as the English School. "The School was indigenous to England, springing from a relation to nature that had always been latent but only now emerged from beneath the fashionable Italian and French classical overlays. The movement was literary, spontaneous, and seems first to have been fired by Sir William Temple's description of the Chinese School (1687). Nature was no longer subservient to man, but a friendly and equal partner which could provide inexhaustible interest, refreshment and moral uplift; irregularity rather than regularity was proclaimed as the objective of landscape design. Lord Shaftesbury's *The Moralists* (1709) lifted the new art into the sphere of intellectual philosophy, revealing that the laws of nature were as universal and unchanging as the Newtonian laws of the heavens, and therefore that the ecology could harmonise with the mathematics of a Palladian mansion."

The Landscape of Man.

30

Hartwell House,
Buckinghamshire.

The circumstances of both these landscapes called for a diametrically different approach. Ditchley was built 1720-22 by James Gibbs as a complete unit of architecture with plans for a classical garden intended as a projection of the house. Fashion changed, formal gardens were "out" and informal "in" and the great terrace presumed to have been made, was demolished and the garden designs were never implemented. It was the spirit rather than the letter of these gardens that was recreated in 1936. Hartwell House, on the other hand, evolved over several centuries, the dominant but by no means the only period being the half-century after Ditchley. Whereas the present day Ditchley designs are static and of one period, those from Hartwell (1980) are a continuum and a veritable tapestry of history.

Hartwell House carries us through the aesthetically turbulent landscape age of Capability Brown to the comparative peacefulness of that of Humphry Repton.

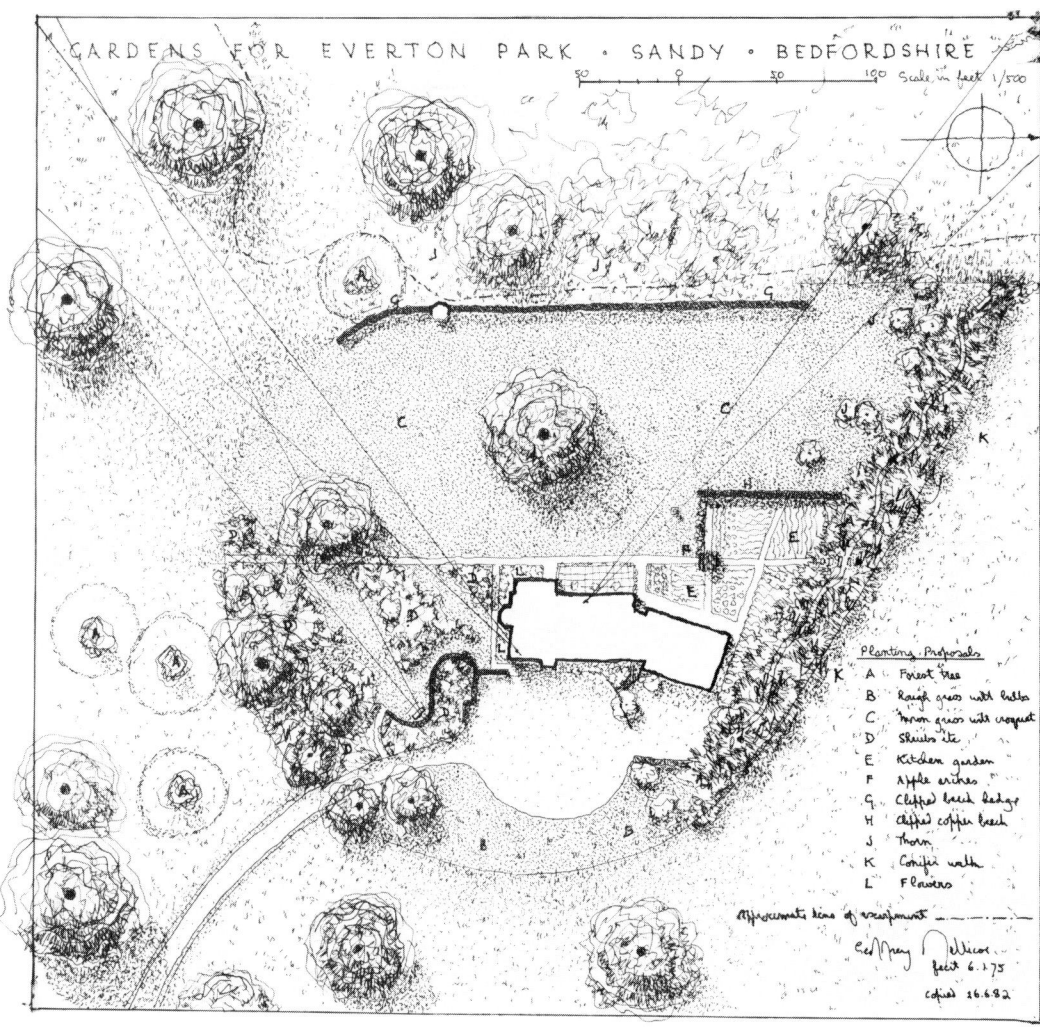

Garden plan, 1974.

Everton Park – BEDFORDSHIRE

Commission: 1974 - 75

Humphry Repton's Red Book on "Hasells Hall in Bedfordshire, a Seat of Francis Pym Esq." is dated 1791. The sketch for the gardens of the new house in the park (now called Everton Park) is dated August 1974 and was made for the Rt. Hon. Francis Pym. A comparison can be made, therefore, between the attitudes of two landscape designers, nearly two centuries apart, towards the home of the same family.

The original eighteenth century brick mansion, now damaged by fire, was built round a central court on the edge of an escarpment facing west over the Bedfordshire plain. The front elevation looked over a flat plateau to the east and south, the west and north being protected from the open landscape both climatically and physiologically by service quarters and stable. To take advantage of the dramatic view, while keeping it in proportion to the whole, the architect had designed a long terrace of such grandeur that even Repton, while deploring the then unfashionable geometry, felt that it should be retained.

View looking south of house, garden and Reptonian trees. Beyond the house is the "disorder".
On the left, the copper beech hedge to the kitchen garden.

Repton's main endeavour, through tree planting, was to emphasize such gentle undulations as existed on the plateau, seen from the approach and principal windows.

The new house was built modestly in neo-Georgian style to suit conditions of living after the second world war. It lies on the fringes of the Repton park along the escarpment a few hundred yards from the mansion. The approach is from the east and the north is protected by the service quarters, the domestic views being towards the west and south. Climatically and physiologically the continual presence of the great view over the Bedfordshire plain (now partly industrialised) was overwhelming, and has been closed by clipped hedges, except for specially placed openings. Privacy being paramount, the east is also closed; and by further closing from the north the "feel" of the gardens is directed towards the ruined mansion and its place in history. The design of the garden is intended to balance classical order with natural disorder.

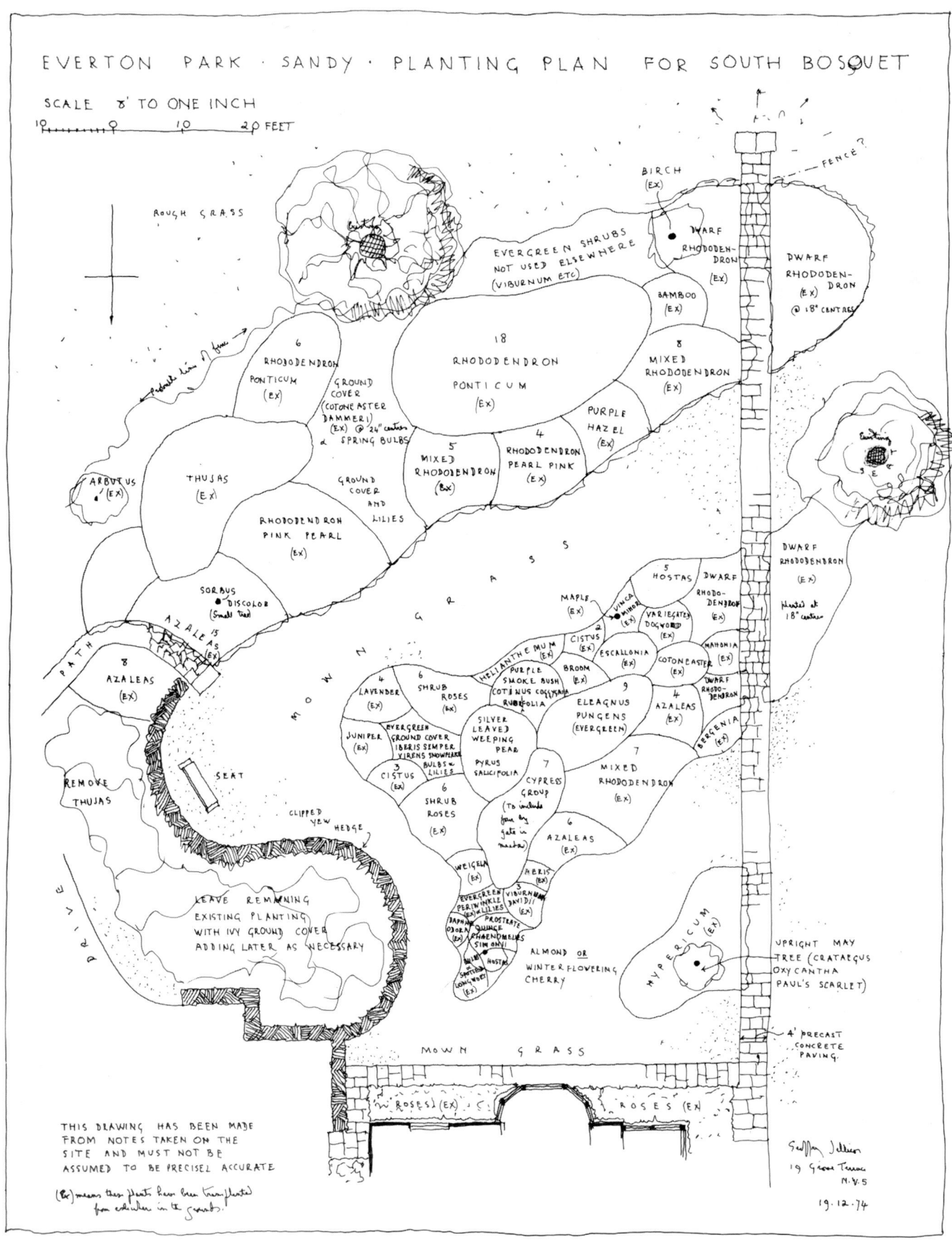

EVERTON PARK · SANDY · PLANTING PLAN FOR SOUTH BOSQUET

SCALE 8' TO ONE INCH

ROUGH GRASS

BIRCH (EX)

DWARF RHODODENDRON (EX)

DWARF RHODODENDRON (EX) @ 18" CENTRES

EVERGREEN SHRUBS NOT USED ELSEWHERE (VIBURNUM ETC)

BAMBOO (EX)

MIXED RHODODENDRON (EX)

6 RHODODENDRON PONTICUM (EX)

18 RHODODENDRON PONTICUM (EX)

GROUND COVER (COTONEASTER DAMMERI) (EX) @ 24" centres & SPRING BULBS

PURPLE HAZEL (EX)

ARBUTUS (EX)

THUJAS (EX)

GROUND COVER AND LILIES

5 MIXED RHODODENDRON (EX)

4 RHODODENDRON PEARL PINK (EX)

RHODODENDRON PINK PEARL (EX)

DWARF RHODODENDRON (EX)

Planted at 18" centres

SORBUS DISCOLOR (Small tree)

5 HOSTAS

DWARF RHODO-DENDRON (EX)

MAHONIA

AZALEAS 15 (EX)

MAPLE (EX)

VINCA MINOR (EX)

VARIEGATED DOGWOOD (EX)

CISTUS (EX)

ESCALLONIA (EX)

COTONEASTER (EX)

DWARF RHODO-DENDRON

8 AZALEAS (EX)

HELIANTHEMUM (EX)

4 LAVENDER (EX)

6 SHRUB ROSES (EX)

PURPLE SMOKE BUSH COTINUS COGGYRIA RUBIFOLIA

BROOM (EX)

9 ELEAGNUS PUNGENS (EVERGREEN)

4 AZALEAS (EX)

BERGENIA (EX)

PATH

JUNIPER (EX)

EVERGREEN GROUND COVER IBERIS SEMPER VIRENS SNOWFLAKE

SILVER LEAVED WEEPING PEAR PYRUS SALICIFOLIA

REMOVE THUJAS

SEAT

3 CISTUS (EX)

BULBS & LILIES

7 CYPRESS GROUP (To include four by gate in masters)

7 MIXED RHODODENDRON (EX)

CLIPPED YEW HEDGE

6 SHRUB ROSES (EX)

6 AZALEAS (EX)

DRIVE

LEAVE REMAINING EXISTING PLANTING WITH IVY GROUND COVER ADDING LATER AS NECESSARY

WEIGELA (EX)

IBERIS (EX)

EVERGREEN PERIWINKLE & LILIES

VIBURNUM DAVIDII (EX)

DAPHNE ODORA

PROSTRATE QUINCE CHAENOMELES SIMONII

BULBS (EX)

HOSTA

SPOTTED LONGWOOD (EX)

ALMOND OR WINTER FLOWERING CHERRY

HYPERICUM (EX)

UPRIGHT MAY TREE (CRATAEGUS OXYCANTHA PAUL'S SCARLET)

4' PRECAST CONCRETE PAVING.

MOWN GRASS

ROSES (EX)

ROSES (EX)

THIS DRAWING HAS BEEN MADE FROM NOTES TAKEN ON THE SITE AND MUST NOT BE ASSUMED TO BE PRECISELY ACCURATE

(Ex) means these plants have been transplanted from elsewhere in the grounds.

Geoffrey Jellicoe
19 Grove Terrace
N.W.5

19.12.74

View of natural disorder, 1982.
The seat for contemplation is concealed even from the house. Behind is the protective yew hedge,
eventually to be over six feet. The seat looks towards the old mansion across a glade soon to be encroached
upon by the "disorder".

◀ Planting diagram of the "natural disorder" 1974 planned to
have continuous unplanned moments of colour.

The Royal Lodge – WINDSOR GREAT PARK

The viewing terrace and bastion from the park.

Commission: 1936-39

In the early nineteenth century the two strands of classicism and romanticism ran parallel in their search to renew a golden past; while John Nash was conceiving Regent Street and the Roman palaces fronting Regent's Park, he was also designing the Royal Lodge in Windsor Great Park for the Prince Regent. The attraction was the dilapidated castle, later transformed by Sir Jeffery Wyattville to outcastle all other pseudo-castles in its grandeur of composition. Since it was built Royal Lodge has undergone many alterations and additions. Set in a beautiful little park within a greater park it has still retained its peculiar classical-romantic charm, now pink and white like an iced cake. In 1936 new gardens immediately adjoining the house were commissioned, and these were designed within the ethos of history.

The viewing bastion.
The timber lions were carved by Allen King, based on the heraldry at Hampton Court.

Wexham Springs

Commission: 1959-61

Transformed from a sedate country house into the centre of the experimental headquarters of the Cement and Concrete Association, the demesne now comprises two nineteenth century estates blended into a single landscape plan.

An unusually imaginative approach to landscape by a commercial company was encouraged by two factors: (1) the recognition that good landscape was good business and that those seeming opposites, plant and concrete, could in fact be happily married; and (b) that only a properly conceived design would be acceptable to the planning authorities. The challenge of design was two-fold: to reconcile technically the tenderness of the flower (the human element) with the concrete (mass-production) and more indirectly to unite the abstract idea of the domestic with that of the superhuman or gigantic — for behind the scenery lay an immense complex of offices, research laboratories and the like, not desiring to loom but equally not to be ignored. The little front terrace to the house, now reception offices, was designed to resolve these differences.

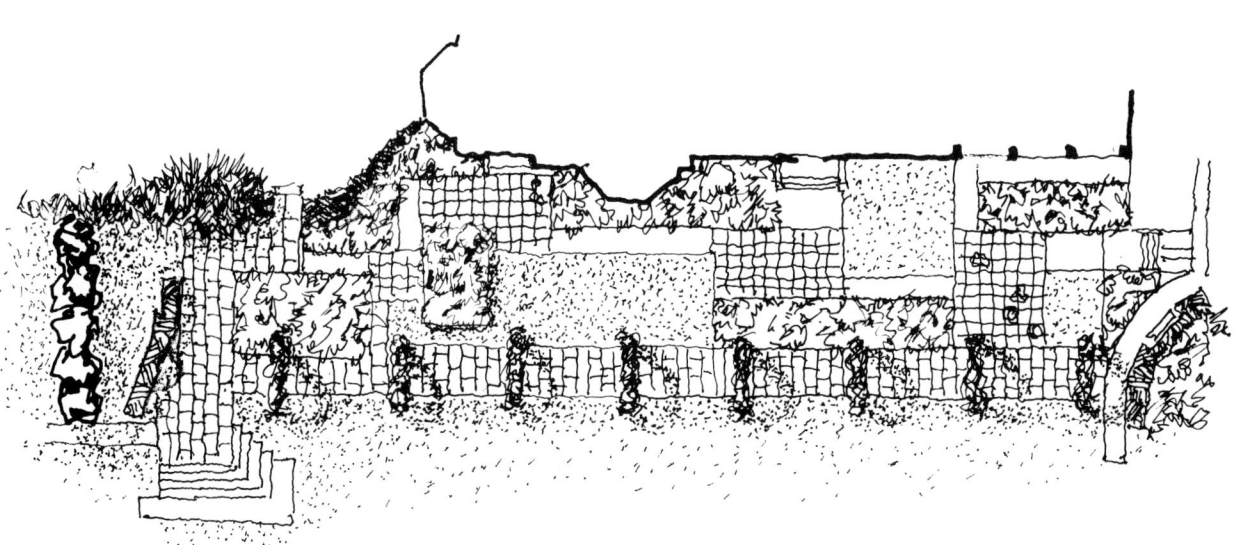

Plan of the terrace showing early influence of the artist Ben Nicholson. The monsters are on the left extremity.

"Provided they are not taken too seriously and are impermanent, there is plenty of room for giants in the modern landscape. One such example is at the research establishment at Wexham Springs in Buckinghamshire...the landscape is in continual change, for it is necessarily experimental. The new terrace garden was laid out with the aim of reconciling past and present, and at one end was placed a great concrete sculpture by William Mitchell.

It is overwhelming, its scale is huge, and it might disappear into dust and dung at any time to make way for another. Without this symbol of gigantic works taking place all around and beyond but outside the picture, the garden composition would have been too gentle and domestic to be influential. As it is, the two quite different philosophies are harmonious. The monsters remain enigmatic and strange, but by no means unfriendly. By the time this book goes to press they may have vanished".

Studies in Landscape Design, Vol. III 1970.

Horsted Place – SUSSEX

Commission: 1965-68/(Uckfield 1956-58)

The present owners moved from Uckfield House to Horsted Place in 1965,
taking with them as the basis of a new garden not only as many of the trees
and shrubs as were moveable, but eleven flower baskets which were to be
incorporated. The baskets were copies of those designed by Humphry Repton
for the Brighton Pavilion. Introduced as special features to the gardens of
Uckfield House, their arrangement differed radically from Repton's own
conception of the multiple use of objects in space. It was as though each of the
objects which had previously been regarded as inanimate had now acquired a
personality of its own. One more adventurous than the others had in fact
slipped across the ha-ha, into the woods, and out of sight in the view opposite.

42

The baskets as originally placed at Uckfield House.

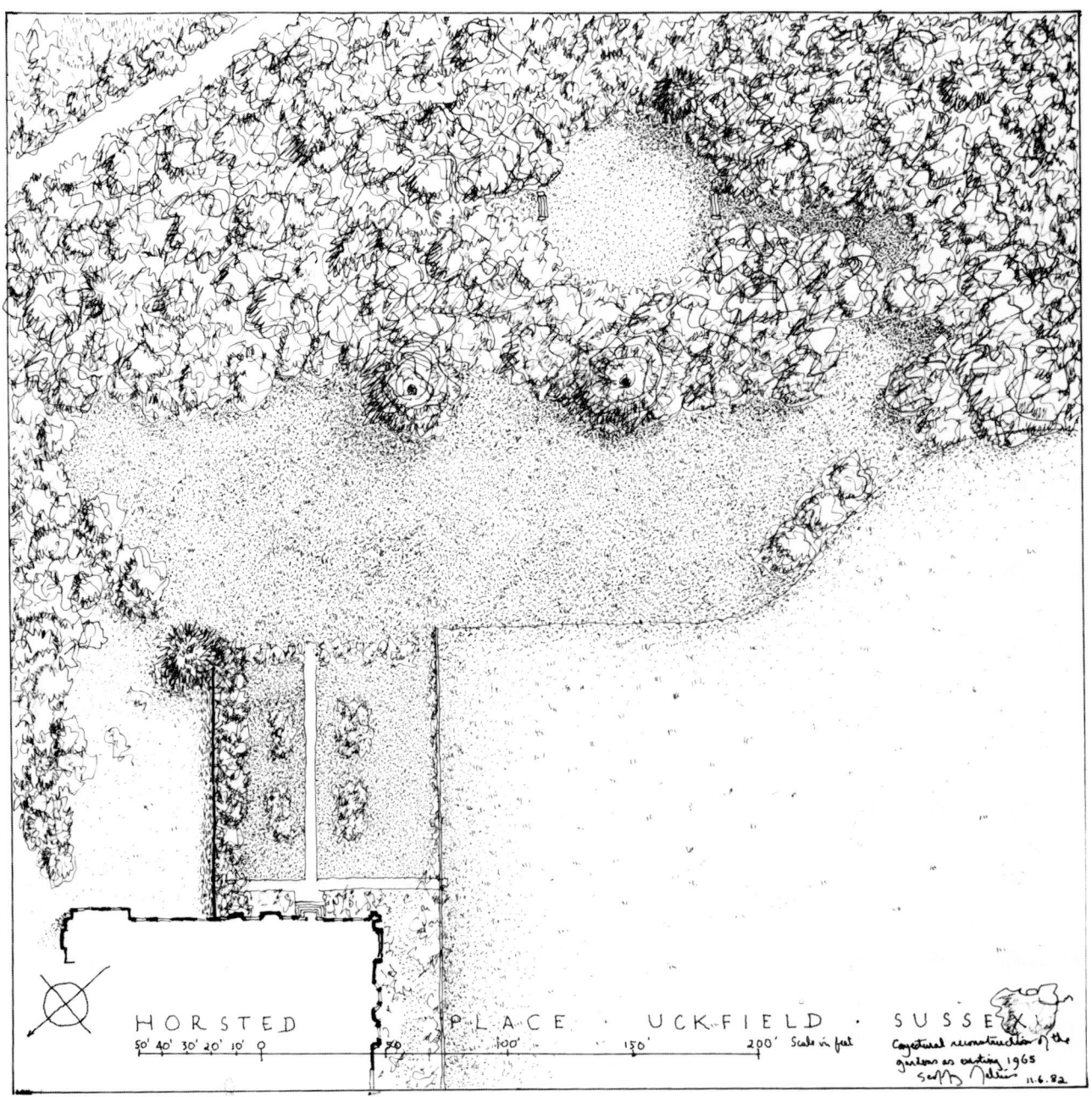

HORSTED PLACE · UCKFIELD · SUSSEX

Conjectural reconstruction of the gardens as existing 1965

Horsted Place —
a site plan as existing 1965.

The house was built in 1852. The internal characteristic is the long green carpeted hall that links east landscape to west, broken in the centre by a white-painted richly carved staircase by Pugin from the Great Exhibition.

Externally the elevations are romantic with a plan that in principle is symmetrical about an axis, having many chimneys and a corner tower. The existing gardens were slight and windswept, but the woodlands to the east were dense enough to hide the London-Lewes road and reduce sound to a low hum. An overhead electricity grid passed across the estate behind the house, and had to be concealed. The garden was designed for the baskets rather than the baskets for the garden. Starting from the house as from a quay these animate objects drift on their green river to disappear into the woods, apparently drawn to the parent circle secreted within.

Horsted Place: gardens 1980. ▶

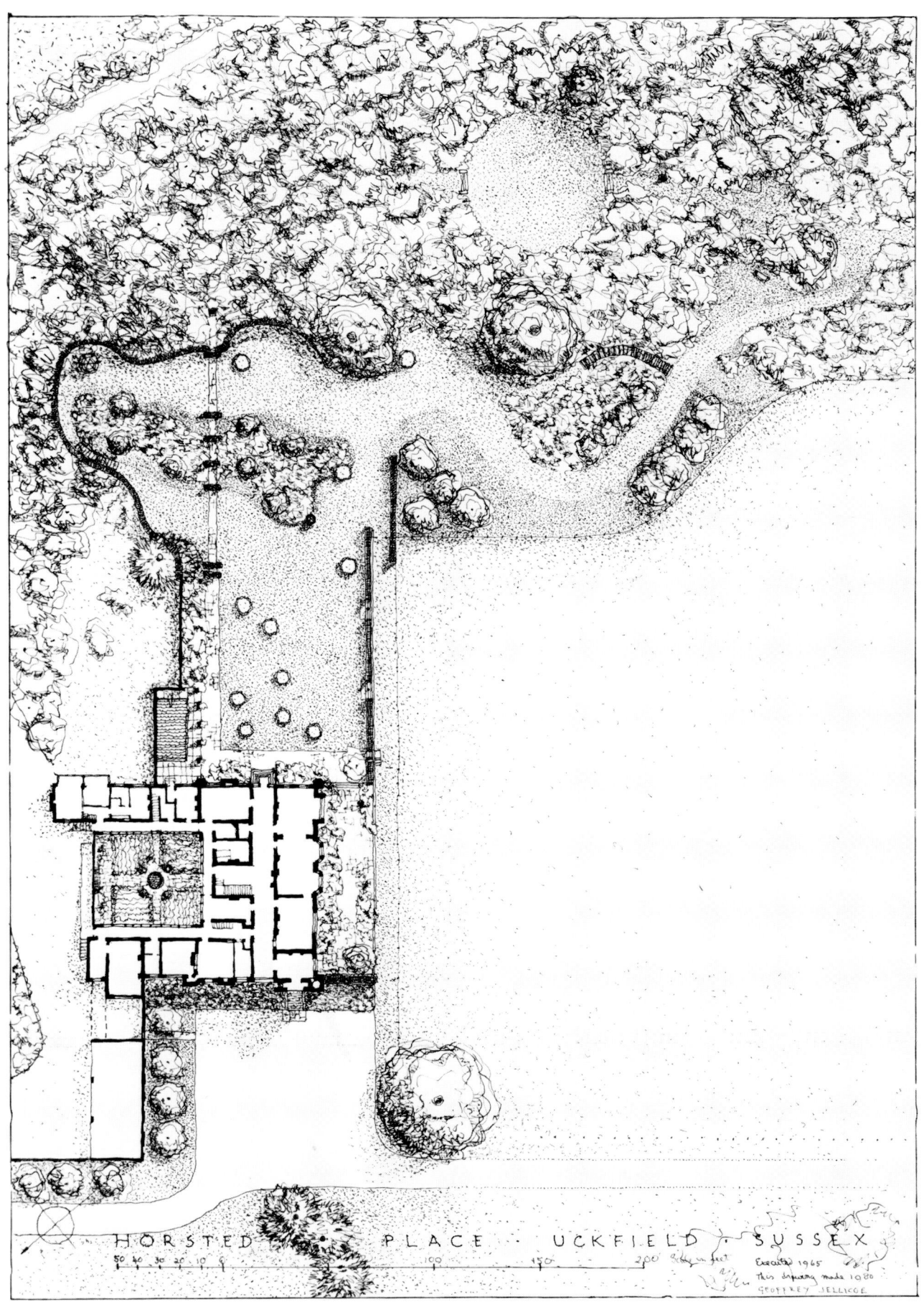

HORSTED · PLACE · UCKFIELD · SUSSEX

50 40 30 20 10 0   100   150   200 Scale in feet   Executed 1965
                                                                        This drawing made 1980
                                                                        GEOFFREY JELLICOE

45

View from the garden towards the east front of the house, showing the starting point of the baskets. The garden had appeared as if by magic. The position of every tree and shrub from Uckfield had been pre-planned, and almost all survived and prospered. The baskets positioned themselves *in situ*.

View from the first floor showing the baskets on their way to the woods.

The grass river looking towards the north where it passes the temple (brought from Uckfield) before returning on itself behind the island on the left. A stray basket is beside it.

To the south the grass circumnavigates a spur of planting, but a short cut through dense foliage penetrates a laburnum tunnel to rejoin it before entering the woods.

Rose Garden in 1962.

Cliveden – BUCKINGHAMSHIRE

The Rose Garden

Commission: 1962

This little garden illustrates the change in man's attitude to environment that has taken place this century – from the nineteenth century's academic outlook to the ecological approach of the twentieth century. Set in the woods of the great classical mansion of 1851 and as if in deliberate contrast to its grandeur, the Edwardian rose garden was redesigned from its geometric circle to correspond with the sensitive feelings of the present owner. The design was inspired by the probings of Paul Klee into the vegetable world.

Planted by its owner, it was never wholly completed, being maintained to-day by the National Trust.

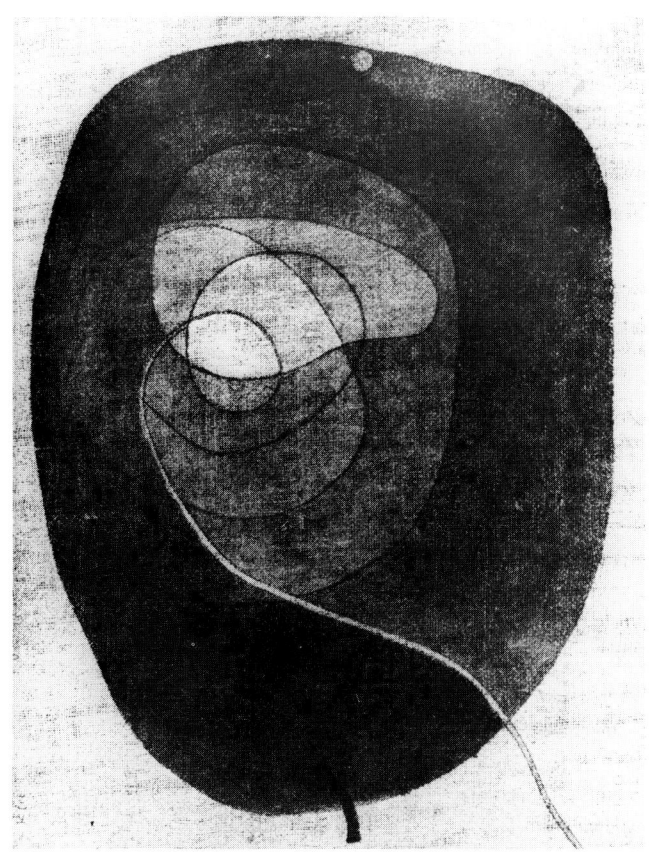

Paul Klee: The Fruit 1932.

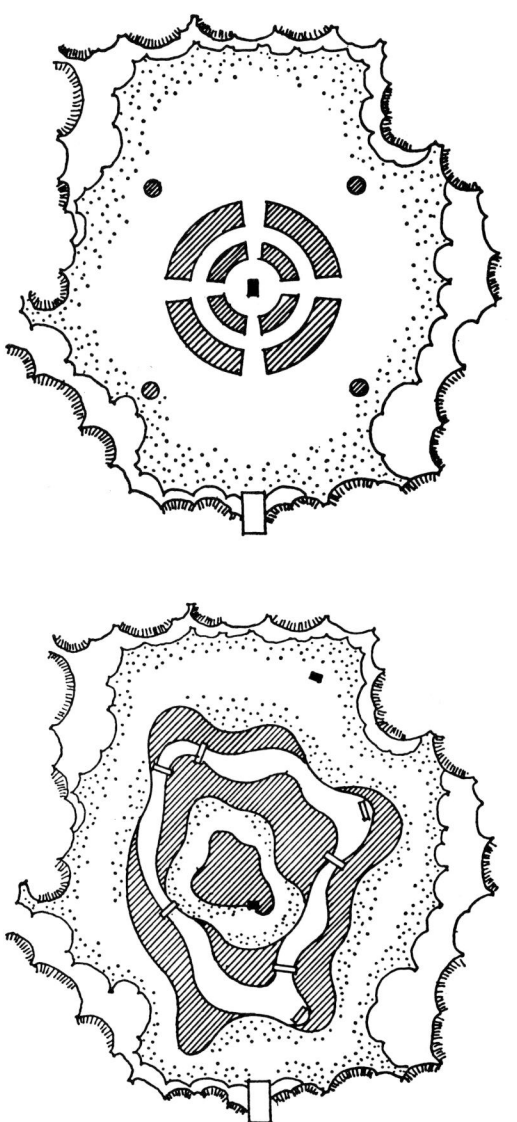

The garden before and after. Apollo remains in the centre.
A Dryad has been rescued from the cellars to follow him forever.

Sandringham House – NORFOLK

Commission: 1947

The four and a half centuries or so of English gardens that separate Sandringham House from Bingham's Melcombe show a wider range of domestic gardens than is to be found anywhere in the world. The cause seems to lie in the variety of the indigenous landscape and its small scale, the unpredictable weather, and perhaps above all in the ethnic medley of the inhabitants. In comparison with other European countries (with the exception of Holland and Scandinavia) all three elements seem to have determined a domestic rather than heroic attitude to the house. After Bingham's Melcombe, and despite an underlying domesticity that refused to be stifled, the urge for grandeur among the leaders of fashion gradually increased until the mid-nineteenth century, a time of which G. M. Trevelyan wrote "the world is not likely to see again so fine and broad a culture for many centuries to come". The most imposing mansion is probably Cliveden, an Italianate palace peculiarly foreign to the basic English temperament. From then onwards a domestic revolt matured in England, brought to a climax at the end of the century by William Robinson and Gertrude Jekyll in gardens and Norman Shaw and Edwin Lutyens in architecture.

The house was built in 1905 as a country residence for Edward VII. It was reasonably far from London, relatively isolated and the shooting was good. In contrast to a Nash terrace in Regents Park which united many houses to give the appearance of a palace, the house itself was a palace concealed within a domestic shell. Within the shell the monarch was allowed to live a private life like any of his citizens. Outside the shell the broad sweep of Edwardian gardens with their patterned bedding-out did not continue the privacy of the interior. In 1947 Edward VII's grandson George VI, coming from the privacy of Royal Lodge to a now almost semi-public environment, determined upon the long enclosed garden that leads across the open lands (like the wall from Athens to the Piraeus) from his study to the woods. In this strictly private garden are still more private "green rooms" of yew. Thus the need for garden secrecy, first demonstrated in the saga of the English home at Bingham's Melcombe, is answered here decisively in the Chinese conception of a box within a box within a box.

The private garden. ▶

Lecture II

THE CREATIVE SUBCONSCIOUS IN LANDSCAPE DESIGN

Introduction

Although the urge of the human psyche to project itself upon its environment is based on a return to the transparencies described in the foreword − Forester, Hunter, Settler − these pictures by themselves are no more than the substance upon which the creative imagination will build. In dreams the creative process of the subconscious can assemble, dis-assemble, and re-assemble pictures in a way that no psycho-analyst has yet been able to direct. But is it not possible to utilise these immense reserve powers of the subconscious to reinforce the more temporal powers of the conscious? One known way is through analogy.

The historic concept that the subconscious can activate the conscious through analogy was first recognised by the Chinese. A Chinese master said to his pupils "never paint even a stone without spirit... if a great mountain is the most important part of your picture, the mountain must seem like a host and the other hills and trees like his guests". In the west, the architect Leone Battista Alberti proclaimed what had long been felt; that architecture and its landscape subsidiaries were based upon the symmetry and proportions of the divinely shaped human body, and that any addition or subtraction would be a disfigurement of the whole. These two contrasting ideas of human behaviour and human form, the one freely ecological and the other strictly ego-centric, amalgamated in the eighteenth century, when the English landscape park encompassed a Palladian mansion.

The door that Edmund Burke opened in *Origins of the Sublime and the Beautiful* has led to the discovery of a vast unexplored and rich geography of the mind. Why, for instance, analogy at all in landscape design? Is it that analogy results from the eternal search for perfection through some perfected object or objects or ideas such as is found only in plant and animal form, the mathematics of the heavens brought to earth in the Paradise garden, or even some classical allegory that has stood the test of time for its completeness and truth? What are the artists dredging up from the subconscious, probings that can release into the landscape some of the greatest ideas within the modern world? and is it an aim, in this psychologically conscious society, to express and balance in the environment not only (as in history) the nobility of man, but his incomprehensible oddities?

Just as the artist cannot make a work of art by intellectual theory alone, so it can be a mistake to make obvious the idea or ideas that he has implanted within the visible, for this would misdirect the flow of idea from subconscious to conscious − and a literary landscape is usually trite. Equally, it may be true that quite unconsciously *all* original designs are inspired by analogy to something known or unknown, post or pre-natal; nothing comes of nothing, and from where else can inspiration come?

Victor Pasmore: *Untitled.*
The drawing is a study of
motion in the abstract.

Harvey's Store – GUILDFORD

The Roof Garden

Commission: 1956-57

It is said that when Kepler discovered that the planets moved around the earth in ellipses rather than circles the new Baroque churches were designed as ovals — an unconscious response to a stupendous event. The impact on the public mind of the launching of the first sputnik in 1956 was equally dramatic. One of the more frivolous spin-offs of this event was the design for the new roof garden of Harvey's Store, high above Guildford. The garden in any case was to be spectacular, the argument being that the public would work their way upwards through the shop and become so exhilarated as to spend money more freely on the way down. The concept took the shape of a sky rather than a terrestial garden, one that would bring to earth the heavenly motions of the planets.

54

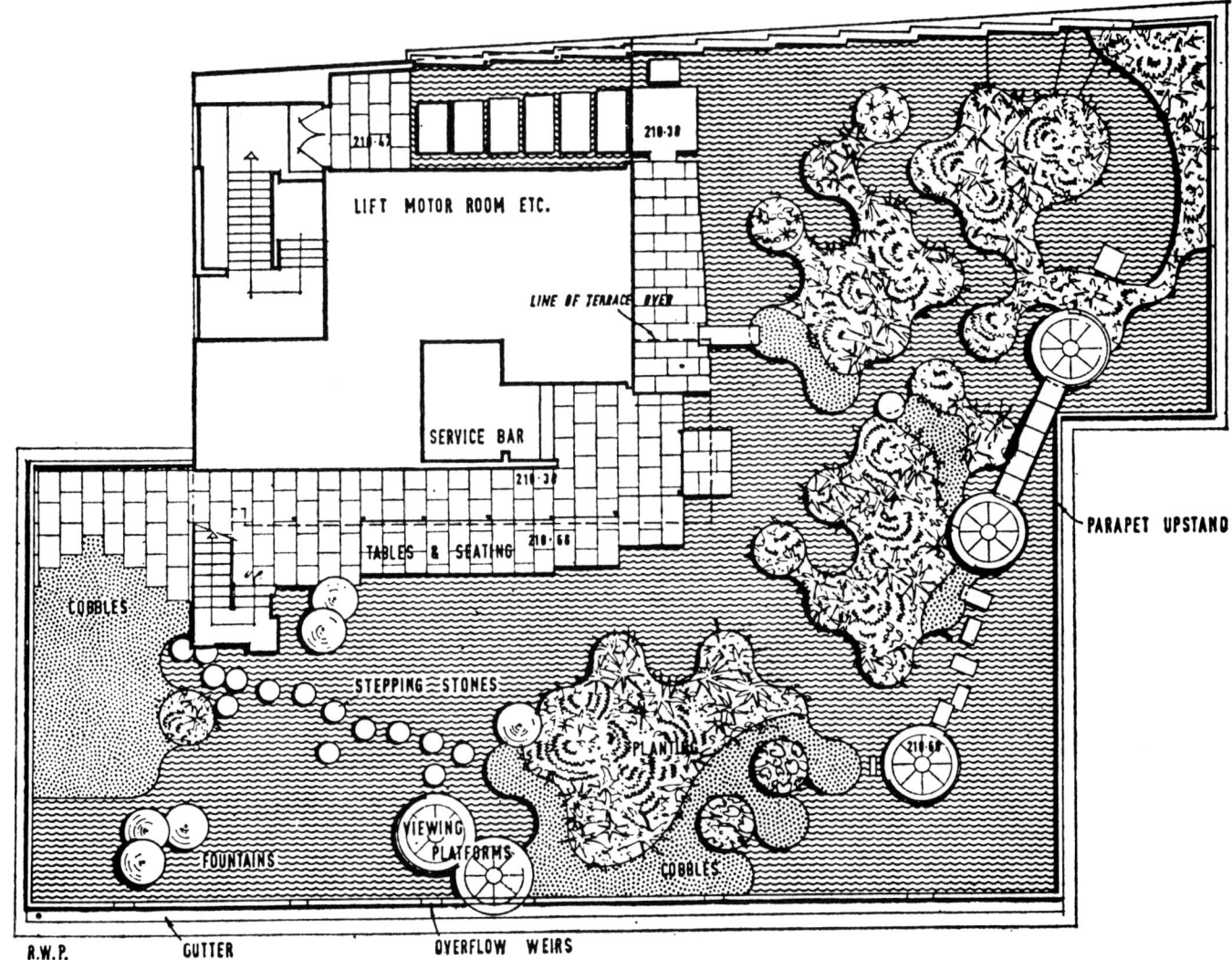

Labels within the plan:

210·42 210·30
LIFT MOTOR ROOM ETC.
LINE OF TERRACE OVER
SERVICE BAR
210·30
TABLES & SEATING   210·68
COBBLES
STEPPING STONES
PLANTING
VIEWING PLATFORMS
FOUNTAINS
COBBLES
210·68
PARAPET UPSTAND
R.W.P.   GUTTER   OVERFLOW WEIRS

Plan as existing 1956.

Roof Garden

The site was some eighty feet above the pavement, with a central block rising higher to cover lift machinery, etc. Since the decision to make something unusual did not come until after the framed structure of the building itself was complete, anything exceeding the calculated live load must come above the stanchions. The idea of flooding the whole to a depth of 9 inches presented no problems. The floor was covered with one extra layer of asphalt, and the islands placed freely on top. The plan is based on standard quadrants, interlocked apparently by self-determination, but easily set out with open joints, on a squared grid. The plants were naturally water loving, the soil mounded above the stanchions to take small trees. The universal problem of evaporation being solved, that of wind called forth the semi-open screen that swept across the site like a cloud shadow. There have been changes since the photographs were taken.

Roof Garden

Upon emerging from the security of the shop below you are confronted with the prospect of a hazardous venture. Dare you go forth into this wild sky garden and complete the circuit with all its excitements and dangers?

You have reached an objective, but what lies ahead? See overleaf.

Here is the test of courage: a river that flows into the sky and is crossed only by stepping stones that are unreal because they float on the water. Will they sink under your weight or carry you off over the edge to eternity. See overleaf.

The Crossing.

"It is the Chinese garden that gives us the most hints on that variety of sensations the experience of which the human curiously enjoys. At Harvey's there is the sensation of adventure and peril, of surprise and the unexpected, of pleasure in accomplishment, of the feel of wet and dry, and above all the modified excitement of being part of an environment that is removed from the every day and is faintly heroic, like the abode of the gods. There are in fact no apparent boundaries; you can fall a sheer eighty feet to the ground. To leave the paved areas is an adventure. You must skip from stepping-stone to stepping stone where a slip will cause you to drown; then you must pass near what the ancients would describe as the edge of the world. To reach the second level (a Valhalla concealing the lift machinery and water tanks) you must pass up a stair suspended in the air. And so forth. Yet these enjoyable sensations are inadequate as part of landscape without their subservience to

Looking back from the ascent.

the second but primary idea of a sky garden. The garden was designed at the time when the first sputnik spun miraculously round and far above the earth, and it was probably the implication of this that caused the whirl of circles that is reminiscent of the planets. Throughout there is constant play upon illusion, whether it is that the stepping-stones apparently float like lotuses upon the surface of the water or whether it is that the water scenery does really join with the sky where it passes out of the scene to the west."

Studies in Landscape Design, Vol. II, 1966.

Paul Klee: Highways and Byways 1929.

Hemel Hempstead Water Gardens

In the eighteenth century the influence on landscape design of such painters as Claude Lorrain, Nicolas Poussin, Salvator Rosa and Rubens was direct. The paintings were intelligible to all, at times so realistic that both Joshua Reynolds and Humphry Repton gave warning that it was unwise to try to interpret a picture literally into landscape. Not only were the media of paint and nature different, but one was static and the other in motion. Nor, in many ways, was the most realistic painting actually real, for the painter, for instance, always places foreground and distance in simultaneous focus, a feat beyond the power of the eye in its assessment of distance. It was not therefore apparent realism that made a landscape painter respected, but the qualities of the abstract that lay behind the figurative. It is contact with this abstract that is a difficulty of to-day, for the revelations of the modern artist from the underworld of the subconscious, richer and more complex that at any time in history, have to be sifted even by the initiated before they can be understood.

Paul Klee: The Vessels of
Aphrodite 1921.
Klee Foundation Bern.

The two paintings suggest the simple visible world of town planning and the
complex invisible world that lies within it and can be called upon to enrich it.

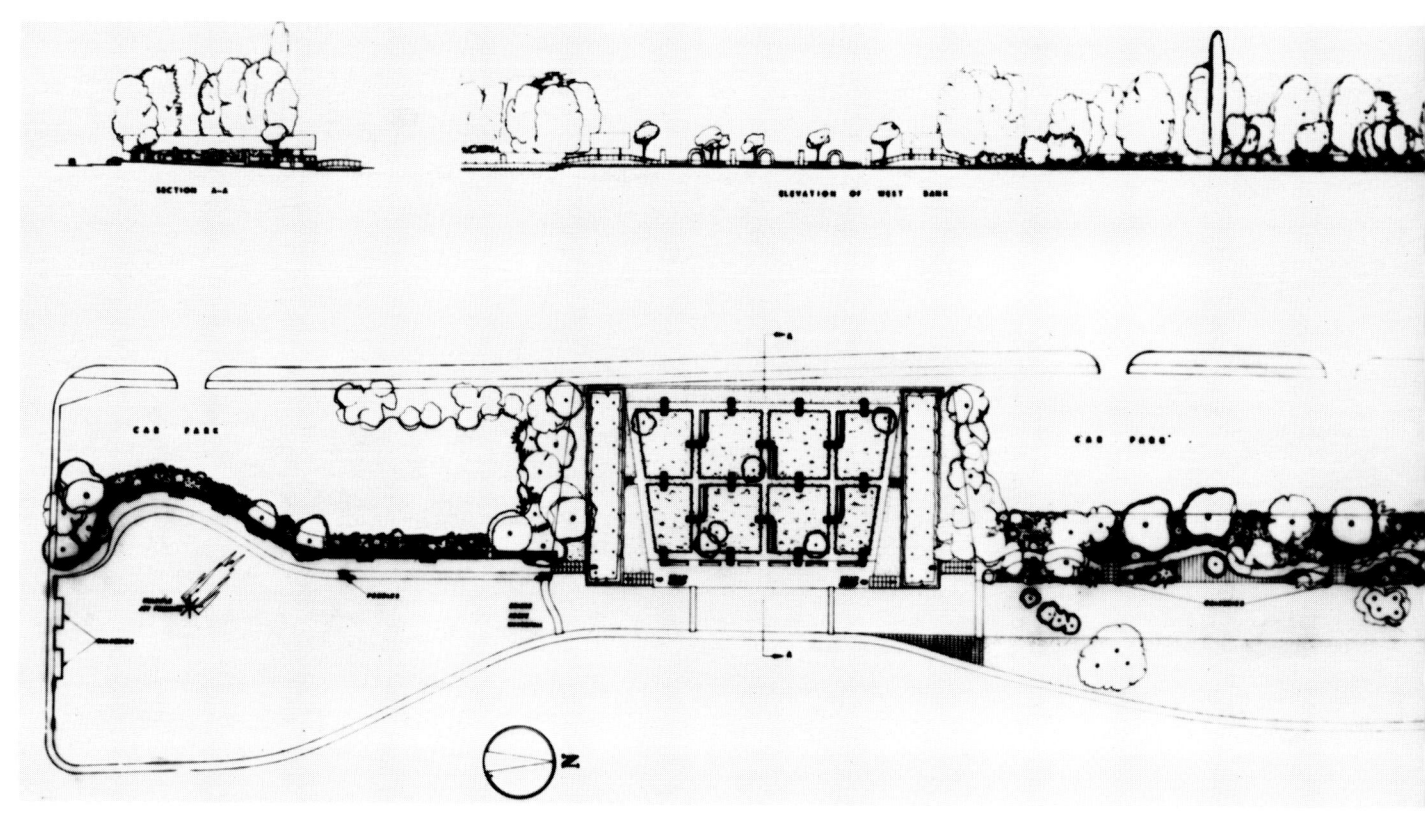

Hemel Hempstead

Plan of the water gardens

Commission: 1957-59

The new town of Hemel Hempstead was designated in 1948 and the water gardens designed nine years later as a public park. The site was a narrow, uninviting strip along the little river Gade, squeezed between the town centre and car parks. It was clear that in order to make any impact upon its urban surroundings it must simultaneously be authoritative and romantic (two normally opposed objectives). The straight line of a canal appeared early in the sketches, widening at the south end into a lake. Excavations from the canal were to be used to conceal a car park and create both the sloping flower

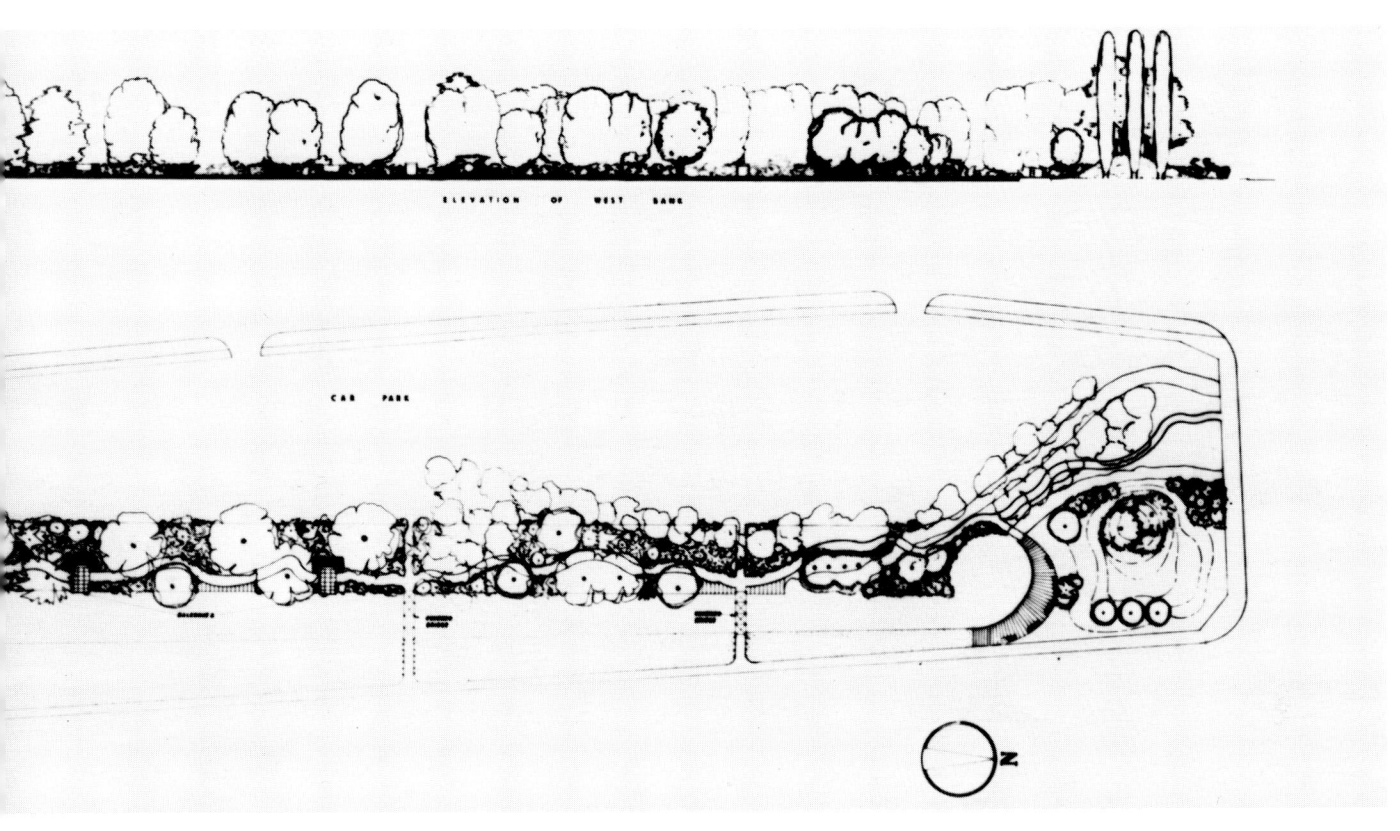

ELEVATION OF WEST BANK

CAR PARK

gardens and the narrow "lovers' walk". The canal was to be dammed with pleasant little cascades and crossed by elegant bridges to give access from car park to town centre. It was then that the serpent, inspired by Klee's two paintings in rich combination, was conceived as a complete and balanced natural form. Thereafter every detail conformed to this idea; the monster head with its single fountain eye and mouth; the flower gardens like a "howdah" strapped to its back; the underbelly curving almost imperceptibly; the lively tail pressing against a hill − all so abstract as to remain unrecognisable and unseen to the roving eye.

Photo 1959

The seen: View across lake from south extremity near water exit. In centre, the multiple jet fountain. To right the rear of the town centre. On left earth mounding to provide provisional cover to car park during growth of beech hedge. In the middle, entrance to canal under bridge connecting gardens and car park to town centre.

The unseen: View across serpent's head from near the mouth. In centre, the eye. In far centre the neck is seen with one of the straps holding the "howdah" across the body.

Photo 1959

The seen: The north extremity of the canal. The diminishing width gives the illusion of length, and the turn to avoid the hill gives the impression of the continuity of a river.

The unseen: The serpent's tail rests against the hill.

Photo 1962

The seen: The lovers' walk. On the right the canal and rear of town centre. On the left the planted mounding concealing the car park.

The unseen: The tufted back contrasting with the plain underbelly with its imperceptible curve, seen on the right.

Photo 1962

The seen: The lovers' walk has two water balconies, but at times the path touches the water. On the left, an island.

The unseen: Children sport with this amiable monster.

Photo 1982

Twenty five years on, 1982, it is possible to assess whether the subconscious idea can project itself into the future when nobody is aware that such an idea exists. The view of the lake from the south shows that the monster's eye is not quite so alert. Two islands have appeared and an attractive bronze sculpture. These additions do not substantially alter the form: the islands become skin reticulations and the two bronze figures dancing on the surface of the water are like flies. The fountain eye can be rejuvenated at any time. Elsewhere the trees on the west bank tend to overhang the canal sufficiently to reduce its apparent size: but the imagination can recreate the form beneath. Trees have been added to the east bank and by linking one side of the canal with the other could, in time, harm the idea of contrast between the two banks.

There are few works so liable to suffer change as parks and gardens. By burying an idea into the water gardens it is hoped that this idea will be its own protection. The form subconsciously aspires to animal perfection and any threat of amputation or deformation would undoubtedly be resisted by the layman, without knowing the reason why.

Photo 1982

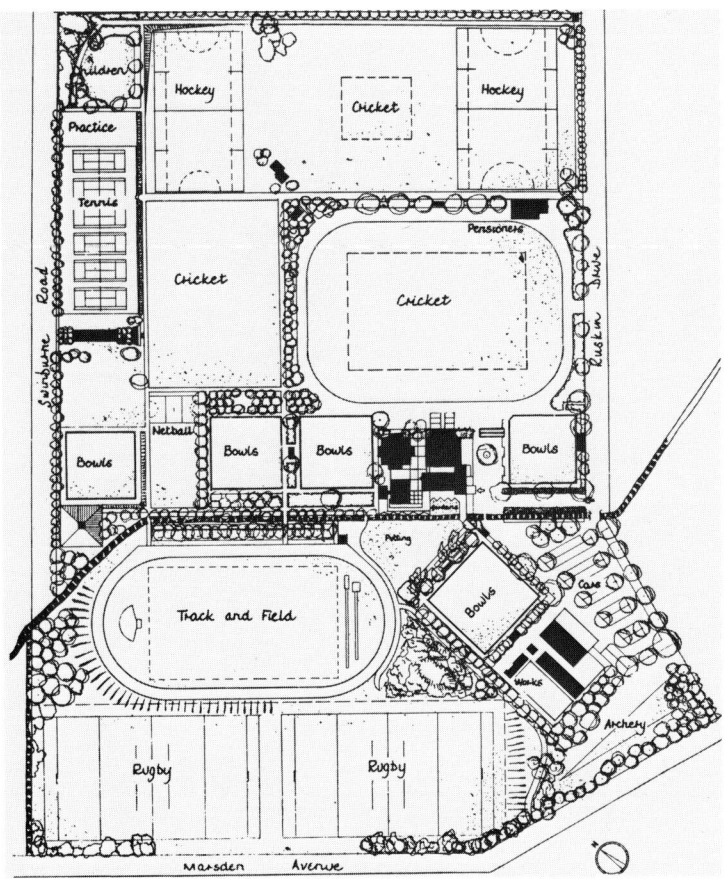

Ruskin Drive Recreation Ground

ST. HELENS LANCASHIRE

Commission: 1957-58

The following was written in 1958 and is taken from Chapter VII:
Studies in Landscape Design, Vol. I, 1960,
"Scale, Diversity and Space."

In an article in the Sunday Times (9.9.58.) entitled "The Goal of Fulfilment" Sir Julian Huxley wrote:

'We must combat everything that threatens the variety of interest needed for human fulfilment – the extermination of wild life, over mechanization, the boredom of mass-production and conformity, the spoiling of natural beauty, the destruction of cultural traditions'.

Ruskin Drive is the name given to the principal open-air recreation centre of a firm of manufacturers in the north of England. The firm, with 14,000 employees in this town alone, is the largest privately-owned business in Europe. The employees are skilled craftsmen working within the framework of what are essentially methods of mass production. Each employee contributes about two-pence a week to the central recreational club and it is estimated that about two thousand were active users of Ruskin Drive before the present alterations and additions.

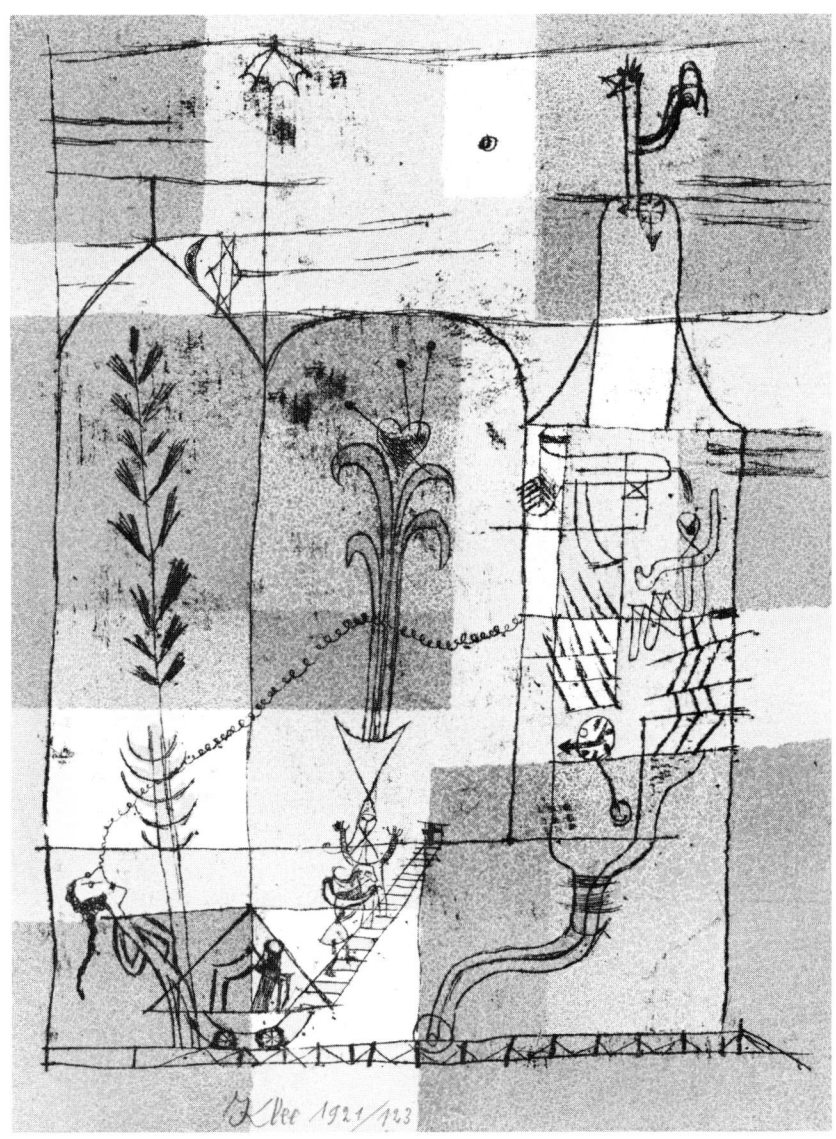

Paul Klee: Scene from
a Hoffman-like tale.

The individual clubs are as follows: archery, badminton, bowls, cricket, football (Association), football (Rugby League), football (Rugby Union), harriers and athletics, horticulture, hockey, judo, netball, rifle, rounders, table tennis, tennis.

It was found that for practical reasons the majority of clubs could best be based upon a central group of buildings, but there were exceptions. The tennis club wished for autonomy, the pensioners desired to be detached, and two cricket clubs required their own shelter pavilions. In addition there was to be a children's play area and a groundman's works area, both remote from the central group. The existing clubroom and cricket pavilions (correctly facing north-east) and the existing changing rooms were too substantial to demolish, even if this were desirable; and it was inevitable that the considerable new club room should be sited behind the old pavilion to face south towards and not away from the sun. The works area which had previously been at the rear was transferred to a redundant bowling green, the turf of which became a turf nursery. The placing of the new pitch was geometrically inevitable.

Ruskin Drive Recreation
Ground. View overlooking
one of the cricket pitches.
In the foreground, children's
climbing sculpture by
John Bridgeman.

It is at this period that the landscape architect pauses to consider quite objectively the underlying idea behind this project. The process of analysis is as follows:

1. The pattern is primarily one of a diversity of clubs, formed for a specific purpose.

2. But these clubs are part of a larger scene whose purpose is very much wider than that of the playing of games, namely to comprehend and bring together agreeably and equally as many individuals as possible.

3. The landscape pattern arising from this would appear to be a basic geometry representing the clubs and their playing fields dispersed into a scene that is near to nature, apparently informal, and yet a comprehensive whole.

4. The core of the pattern is the club house and its particular landscape where all can meet. This is a kind of inner precinct, a Chinese box of landscape within another box.

Ruskin Drive Recreation
Ground. Children's play area.

5. From this the landscape designer will quickly assess the qualities of the
existing landscape that should be emphasized or suppressed. Generally
speaking the environment of houses is excluded, but a view across adjoining
open land is encouraged as an extension of space. The canal sets the geometric
pattern and must be idealised from what is really no more than a useful drain.
The building to be retained acquires a historic flavour. The pattern of grass
and trees on the north side remains unchanged, but the flowers are moved
into the precinct.

In his struggle to obtain a hold on feeling, Klee is almost contemptuous of
intellect in the modern world. The appeal to the subconscious is paramount.
An example of his work which has had some influence on the Ruskin Drive
design is the "Scene from a Hoffman-like Tale" 1921. Here in fact this painter
has superimposed one idea upon another, diversity upon space; and here
above all is the sense of friendliness, warmth and unity that Huxley must have
had in mind when he wrote the article quoted at the beginning of this study.

Rutherford Laboratory – HARWELL

Commission: 1960

In his own search for the origins of man, Henry Moore has probed inwards beyond intellectual man, animal man and man the vegetable, beyond all individual oddities and peculiarities, to that period when living matter derived from rock and water. It is this grand concept that informs Moore's sculpture, evoking a sense of the dignity and agelessness of the human race. His influence on myself began in 1927, finding eventual expression in the lake landscape of 1980 described in Lecture IV.

Henry Moore: Draped Figure 1952-53. "There is no other sculptor who will be such a source of inspiration to those future generations of landscape designers who will be called upon to model the land" *(Studies in Landscape Design, Vol. II, 1966).*

Henry Moore:
Draped Reclining Figure.

Henry Moore: King and Queen on the moor at Shawhead, Scotland.

Harwell's subterranean laboratories are concerned with high-energy atomic research. Above them was a huge waste heap of excavated chalk which was to be remodelled to fit the existing landscape at the foot of the Berkshire Downs. The scientists will tell you that the splitting of the atom leads to infinity, or (as one of them said) to "God". Be this as it may, the project was named "Nimrod", the mighty hunter and scourge of mankind. As if to act as guardians of this underground monster, three hills were placed upon it and named: Zeus, father of gods and man; Themis, one of his wives, divine justice, daughter of heaven and earth, goddess of law, justice and order; and their daughter Klotho, one of the fates who determines the life and death of man. The assurance was that so long as Klotho remained constant, the future of man was safe. But this was not to be . . . for shortly before the start of work a telephone call stated that the small hill, Klotho, would impede certain rays emanating from Nimrod and must be removed. So Klotho was returned to

Rutherford High Energy Research Laboratory, Harwell. The chalk waste of 350,000 cubic yards before remodelling.

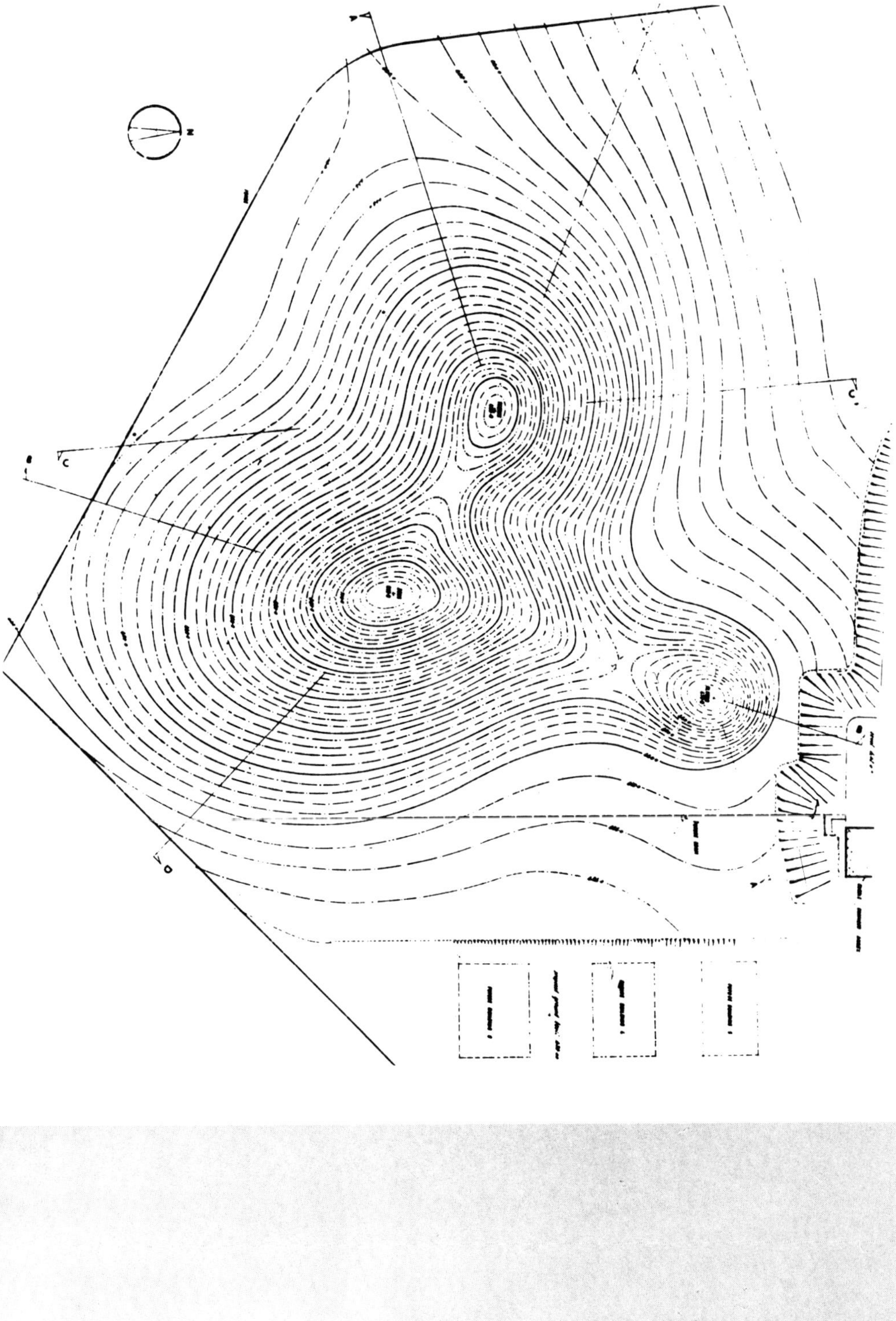

Plan of the three hills as
first designed.

Model of three hills.

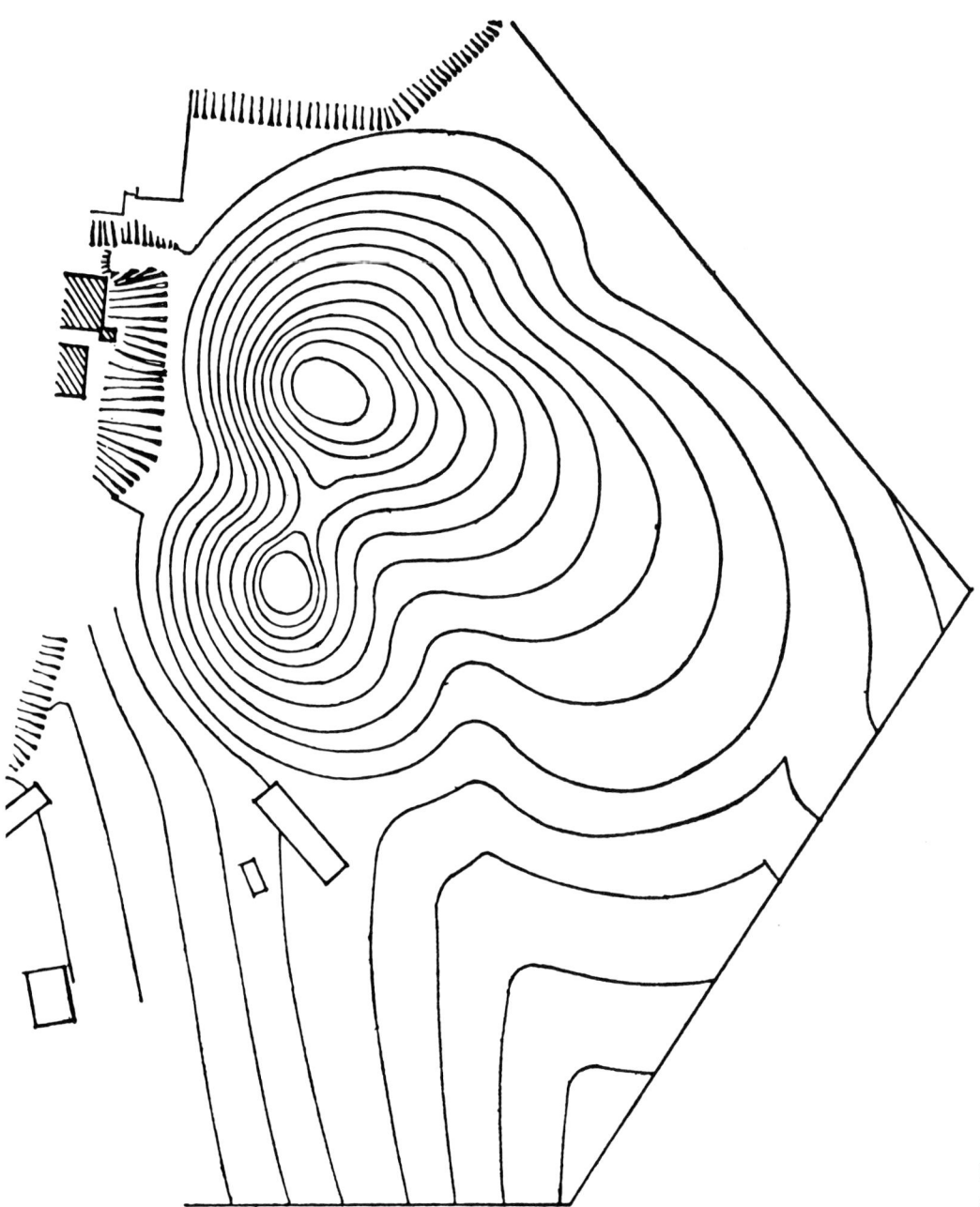

Harwell: the executed design
showing only two hills.

Themis's womb and only the two hills of Zeus and Themis were made. The fate of mankind therefore, still hangs in the balance… "The execution of these hills is revealing. The drivers of the bulldozers were unable to fashion the contour to the designer's precise drawings. The contractors, in despair over the time schedule of their contract, appealed for help. I went immediately to Harwell, explained directly to the men that I was interested in spirit rather than fact, pointed to the "sweet" concave and convex curves of the adjoining Downs on which their families must have picnicked and left them to it. The contract was completed quickly and to the special satisfaction of the landscape artist who made no changes. The men had become part of the design process, and had known it".

(Studies in Landscape Design, Vol. II, 1966)

The hills in the making.

The completed hills.

Oldbury-On-Severn Nuclear Power Station

Ben Nicholson:
Painted Relief 1943-4.

GLOUCESTERSHIRE

Commission: 1960

In the foreword, the phases of the subconscious have been likened to a series
of transparencies laid one upon another. The deepest is rock water and
vegetable, then comes forest man, then man the hunter, and finally quite
recently in evolutionary time, the settler with his discovery of geometry as a
necessity for survival. The Egyptians began the transformation of geometry
from a science into an art, and the Greeks brought the art to earthly
perfection, fully aware (as Plato accepts) that the goal of absolute perfection is
out of reach to humanity. Greek proportions underlie western classical art,
disappearing and re-appearing as the fashion changed from classicism to
romanticism and vice-versa. In the twentieth century Piet Mondrian reached
the ultimate austerity in mathematical art, but at the sacrifice of biological
form and those idiosyncrasies without which man cannot survive. It was left to
Ben Nicholson to evolve an abstract geometry that accepted terrestial
limitations while bringing to earth the majesty of the heavens with their
absolute balance and order. My own association with him began in 1963 and
continued without interruption until its culmination in the 1980 Wall described
in Lecture IV.

Ben Nicholson: Olympic Fragment, June 1963.

Air view of site 1960.

The landscape design was commissioned by the Central Electricity Generating Board as a pilot guide to consortia competing for the construction of the whole project.

Included in the terms of reference was the disposal of two million yards of subsoil from the river bed (excavated to form a tidal reservoir of cooling water) so as to form a plateau on the adjoining land. The following is from *Studies in Landscape Design, Vol. II:*

"The philosophic purpose of the design is to provide a link between the small irregular pattern of the flat low-lying fields and the vast bulk of the station itself. The first expresses a world that is rapidly passing, of shapes haphazardly rising from random land ownership and land cultivation; it is a pattern that is excessively unscientific and on this account human and friendly. The power it expresses is that of the horse, although the tractor is more apparent in the modern world. The hedgerow trees are also haphazard, but provide shelter for cattle and protection from wind; the hedgerows are alive, as are the fields, with a complex of animal and vegetable life. Upon this pattern is imposed a foreign element that is literally monstrous for it is

The pilot design.

concerned with wresting power from the universe itself. It is wholly mechanical and scientific, has no relation to its human environment, and the power that it produces is exported along overhead wires to remote and populous regions. There is nothing that the architect can do to humanize these buildings, even if he wished to do so. The part to be played by the environment is therefore paramount, for it must act as a link and reconcile two very conflicting ideas."

Let us now, for guidance, turn to the art of Ben Nicholson.

"The question before the landscape architect is whether such a lofty conception of art can be interpreted into physical form and upon such a vast scale. Certainly the philosophic basis of the environment at Oldbury is congenial to such an experiment for here is a profound geometry modified by irregularities which mysteriously enrich the scene".

The plateau was designed in four dimensions, with the agricultural pattern to be in constant change. In the event a miscalculation of soil was revealed during progress of works and the full pattern of the plateau was not realised.

The Kennedy Memorial – RUNNYMEDE

Giovanni Bellini: *Allegory of the Progress of the Soul.*

Commission: 1964-65

John F. Kennedy was assassinated on 22nd November 1963. Within a very short time the British Government designated a parcel of land (an historic "acre") on the slopes above Runnymede as a gift to the United States in memory of one who had dedicated his life to the pursuit of peace throughout the world.

A memorial to a President of the United States following an assassination at the height of his power is a great dramatic idea. It is universal and transcends daily events and personal idiosyncracies. Only through analogy did it seem possible to lift the idea beyond the gentle and modest English countryside in which it was to be set.

The analogy that evolved was that of Bunyan's *Pilgrim's Progress*, one of life, death and spirit. Inspiration for the conversion of this analogy into landscape reality came from two paintings made at the time when civilised man was emerging from the dark ages to observe and record the beauty of the world about him. The *Allegory of the Progress of the Soul* by Giovanni Bellini (1430-1516) shows how pure geometry can create the sublime out of natural landscape.

Giorgione: The *Tempest*.

The *Tempest* by Giorgione Castelfranco (1478-1510) shows how two tangible
elements in a pictorial composition, the human, can create an intangible third
in the imagination.

The model as seen from the meadows.

The site lies on the cold north slopes rising above the flat meadows beside the Thames, where Magna Carta was signed in 1215. On the left in the view are natural self-regenerating woodlands; in the centre, meadowland with thorn trees; behind and above, a clump of Scots pine; to the right, rough copse. The model shows that this peaceful scene is itself the memorial, and what has been fitted into it is no more than a statement of purpose – an intangible idea that is emphasised by the duality of the design, as in the *Tempest*. The approach is

View of site from the meadows as existing 1963.

The model showing calculated duality of composition.

an uphill climb through the woodland on the left in the model. The inscribed stone itself is seen on the edge of the woods; a long path follows the contours; and two seats of contemplation are seen embedded in the hillside between the ancient thorn trees and immediately below the Scots pine. A ha-ha can be seen parallel to, and below, the path, for there must be no apparent barriers between American and British soil. We can now enter this landscape and experience both the *seen* and the *unseen*, the real and the analogy...

The seen: The entrance gate to the memorial landscape is reached across meadowland that at certain times is water logged. Hence the granite setts scattered on a boggy threshold. The meadows and memorial are administered by the National Trust.

The unseen: The Wicket Gate, entrance to the allegory of Life, Death and Spirit. First you must pass through "the Dark Wood" of Dante.

The seen: Some 60,000 axe-hewn granite setts form the path that winds upwards. The surface is intentionally rough, as should be the way of a pilgrimage, but in practice this led to wear on the grass edges, later altered to a hard surface. According to modern forestry practice the woodlands are regenerate and appear uncared for — too many seedlings and too many over-mature trees.

The unseen: The setts are a multitude of pilgrims on their way upwards. No sett is an exact copy of another. Only when the craftsman laying the setts appreciated the analogy could he break away from the uniformity and regimentation to which he was conditioned. The woodlands represent the full cycle of life, this effect of self-regeneration calling in reality for special skills in forestry.

The seen: The setts were normally laid dry, but the risers were purpose-made and set in concrete. There have been some regrettable losses from pilgrims seeking mementoes.

The unseen: The craftsman was unable to interpret the analogy of the unseen until they were compared to the uneven front of a crowd watching a football match.

The seen: Above the steps the monument is seen beside a thorn tree. The setts fan out to receive standing visitors. On the far right are the threshold steps.

The unseen: The awkwardness of the upland journey is a preparation for the tranquility of the stone itself, a catafalque borne on the shoulders of the multitude. The thorn is symbolic, for President Kennedy was a Catholic. Behind the stone is a newly planted American scarlet oak, which is in colour in November.

The seen: The stone weighs seven tons and was carved from a fourteen stone block. It is curved in all directions to correct optical distortion and give impression of a great weight floating above the ground. The threshold steps are from the Roche bed at Portland whose shell markings indicate an age of 150 million years. In the right foreground is a stepping stone from the unmarked St. Pauls bed that leads to the terrace walk. In order to counteract vandalism the stone itself was treated with silicon, which keeps it unweathered. The inscription on it, from the President's inaugural address, reads:

> Let every nation know whether it wishes us well or ill that we shall pay any price bear any burden meet any hardship support any friend or oppose any foe in order to assure the survival and success of liberty.

The lettering is so disposed across the surface that it reads as texture, as though the stone itself were speaking rather than having had an inscription carved upon it.

The unseen: the difficulty of sustaining an analogy is shown by the orthodox "cushion" on which the stone rests, for this should have expressed more clearly to the subconscious the idea of a catafalque resting on the shoulders of the multitude. The view shows the meeting place of all three parts of the analogy of body, mind and spirit. The terrace walk is deliberately detached from the threshold steps to lead into the future, like Jacob's ladder.

The first of the two seats.

The idea of the two seats to symbolise thrones was suggested by Henry Moore's "King and Queen" on the moors at Shawhead in Scotland (page 77). The upper seat, backed by the pines on the skyline, is the public image of the President; the secondary seat, that of his consort. The philosophy of this concept was recorded in a lecture in 1967 to the students of the Royal Academy of Arts.

"The primary contribution the human mind has made to the world is its endeavour to create order out of chaos. It has long been recognised that the underlying order is mathematical and this suggests that geometry is the visual expression of such order. Geometry means proportion and it is a sense of proportion that has created and stabilized the civilization of all ages. For Western civilization the scientific study began with the Greeks, and more especially with Pythagoras. Pythagoras established that the tones in music can be measured in space and Plato later discovered this harmony in geometric form. The pavings are massive and mathematically proportioned and a raked joint is intended to convey the idea that each stone is an element in its own right. The second of the two seats is smaller than the first, is slewed slightly inwards, and has a different stone pattern. This is the King-Queen, man-woman relationship, and you will note the link between the two of a further two stepping-stones, one smaller than the

The two seats of contemplation overlooking the meadows and River Thames, where Magna Carta was signed.

other, and draw upon your imagination for an explanation. The second seat fits the nature of the existing levels and is tucked away privately among the rampant hedges and adjoining mole-hills."

This highly sophisticated and precise design is fitted into a landscape that is very much the reverse. The intention is to convey the same impression as that of a Greek Temple, whose presence lends meaning to a primitive scene... .

It is again the Greek temple that gives a clue in regard to *scale*, for it is aloof and heroic. The steps forming the podium of a temple, are, for instance, gigantic. The reason for this is well illustrated in Bellini's *Progress of the Soul* (page 86) where the scale of the balustrade is superhuman — it is to lift an object from the *actual* to the *idea*. The seats at Runnymede are larger than is normal.

Kennedy Memorial

A recent photograph showing how the necessary increase in granite setts to contain visitors has added dignity to the memorial stone without impairing the analogy. Because of its surface treatment the stone appears unweathered and outside time. In its aetherial sense of weightlessness, the stone is the predecessor of the Nicholson Wall described in Lecture IV.

Lecture III

SPACE/TIME IN LANDSCAPE DESIGN

Introduction

The half-century from 1930-80 saw a transformation in man's relation to environment so swift as to have no parallel in history. The comparable period, before and after 1600 in Italy, was significant in causing the breakdown of accepted faiths. The circle, for instance, that was thought to govern the movements of the planets and informed all that was "good proportion" (Plato's mean and divine proportions and geometrical progression), was not a circle at all, but an oval. Kepler's discovery may have been a metaphysical catastrophe and the cause of an aesthetic revolution, but mathematics as a fact remained absolute, as did Plato. This is not so to-day, when Euclid is disowned, when a unit of time/space exists as a concept that is incomprehensible to the layman, and when art as the traditional bridge between man and the cosmos seems to have broken down.

This lecture attempts no more than to present the challenge of time/space design in terms of landscape. Architecture is a static art, until recently built for eternity (as Wren said) but landscape is in movement the moment it is created. Although it is the youngest of the organised arts and by far the most complex, it can claim to be the only one in harmony equally with the static in architecture and the dynamic in the changing universe of matter.

The way of thought in the thirties clung to that of the seemingly stable Settler transparency, reflected in neo-Georgian architecture. The three studies in this lecture are intended to show the profound change of attitude that has since taken place. The examples progress in scale from the individual home that is common to all, through a comparison of the approach to the design of two similar historic gardens, to one in which the human unit symbolised by the home has become submerged in a gigantic self-creating work of machine art, whose uncontrolled future could dominate our lives and destroy our civilisation.

This thesis of space/time and man's response to it, however, is more than a study of physics alone, for it sets out to ask a question only partially answered by the artists. Lecture IV will argue that provided *all* (metaphorically speaking) aspects of human nature are understood and integrated into the designed environment, would the troubled psyche, as in the past, ultimately be its own saviour in a universe in which self-identity might otherwise disappear?

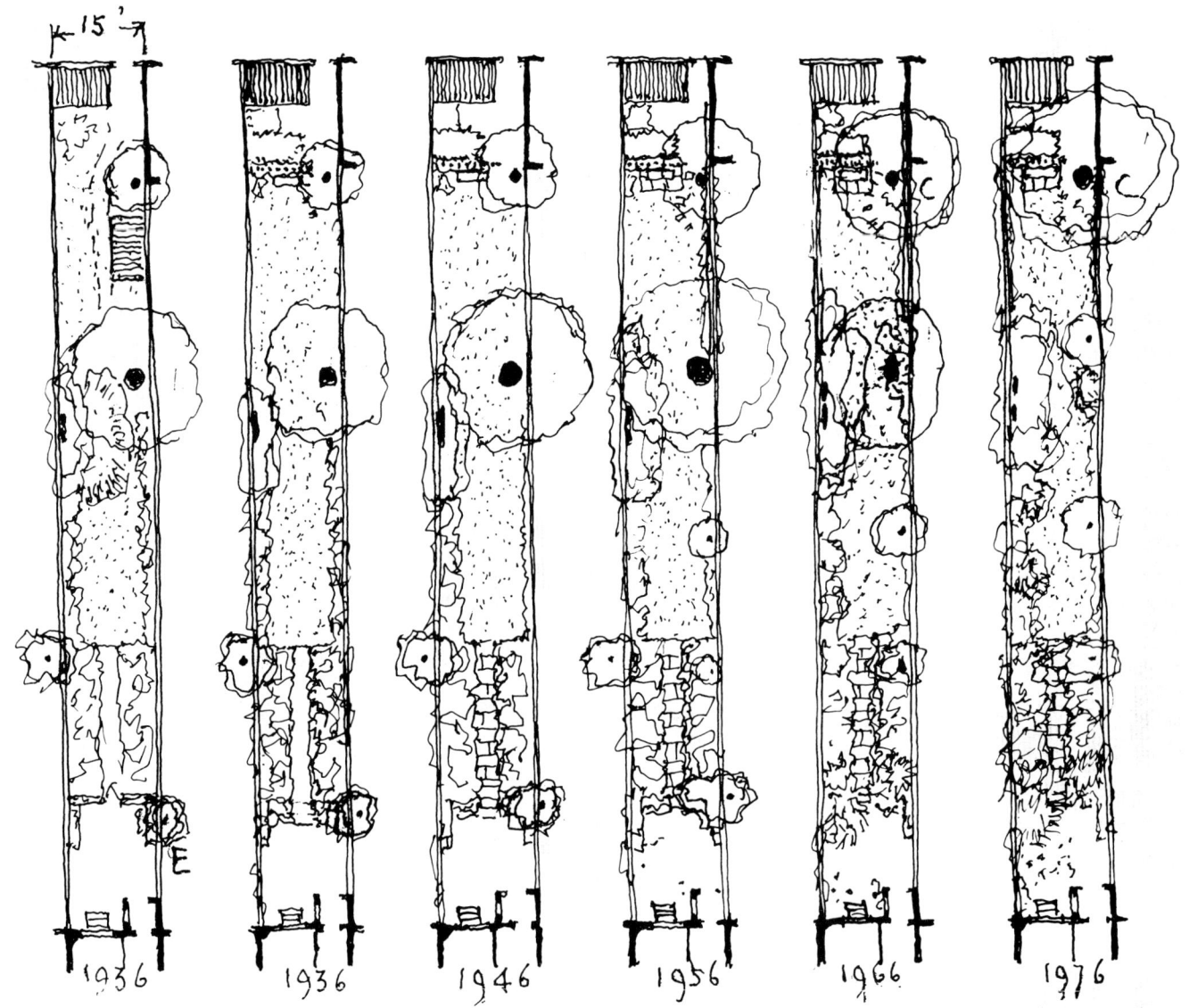

Plans showing five decades of change.

Grove Terrace – HIGHGATE

Commission: 1936-

While architecture remains static, every garden that is not an extension of architecture is in constant change. The obvious changes are seasonal but within the repetitive process there could quietly be taking place a further progressive change that is fundamental. Plants and humans are never static. They can grow up and mature in ways that are equally unpredictable. This town garden in Highgate is a record, experienced over more than forty years, of the way in which the mood of a garden can appear to have changed of its own accord, imposing its changes of idea imperceptibly upon its owners. In art historian terms the change is from the classical to the romantic; the space involved is no more than a rectangle five by fifty paces.

102

The garden in 1938.

The first two plans show the site in 1936 before and after alterations. The existing impedimenta were removed and a long axial lawn passed under and between a mature ash and an old fig tree, to terminate architecturally on a white seat against a formal trellis. The view of 1938 shows the firmness of the enclosing walls and their underlying geometry, but suggests also an element of mystery in the far distance − a sense of mystery that was eventually to advance up to the house itself. The exceptional length of the gardens allowed forest trees to conceal the opposite houses; behind the ash is seen a young self-sown sycamore that would in time take the place of the older tree in the composition.

Early summer 1956

When the fig leaves are out the light reflecting object in the opposite houses will disappear.

Spring 1976

The view shows the changed structure of the garden. The ash has gone and its place in the composition been taken by the sycamore. The fig tree will soon reach across to the opposite wall. Shrubs have taken the place of herbaceous plants and the walls are planted out and will disappear in high summer.

High Summer 1976

The transformation from an open to an enclosed garden is complete. The garden end has become a *giardino segreto*.

The illusion that carries humanism into the heart of nature lasts only a few months. Before the leaves fall and there is disillusionment, it is possible to lie on the ground and looking upwards to the sky through fig or sycamore leaves (or both) to imagine a return to forest origins and the processes of nature.

Note: the sycamore disappeared in March, 1983.

Ditchley Park

Commission: 1936-38

and

Hartwell House

Commission: 1979

The garden in Grove Terrace is a microcosm of the gradual change of attitude towards environment that took place quite unconsciously between the thirties and the eighties. Seen side by side, a comparison of the plans for Ditchley Park made in 1936, with those of Hartwell House, made in 1979, show even more decisively the difference in the approach to landscape design. The difference is crystallised in the conservationists' query "whose time is this place?", the answer to the one being a date in the past, to the other in the present.

The two great houses differ in as much as Ditchley was built at one time, while Hartwell was built over the centuries. Geographically they are within a carriage drive of each other, and at the most evolutionary time in English landscape history were both owned by the same family. The Lees called in the architect James Gibbs, first to build the one and then interest himself in the other. The cause of Gibbs' change of thought towards environment that took place between these two works curiously parallels what is happening in the present century; the revelation of a new, unbounded and hitherto unknown conception of space. To understand this we must follow Gibbs to Rome where he worked for two years in the Bernini-influenced office of Carlo Fontana. Rome at that time was in what can best be described as a spatial ferment. Bernini had broken the doctrine of classicism that accepted an object as complete in itself and found in Baroque an idea that regarded space *between* objects (in Bernini's case, sculpture) as having its own significance. To Gibbs with his traditional classical background this concept must have been overwhelming. On returning to England he became one of the fringe of the Burlington circle, the inspirers of the English Landscape School with its revolutionary ideas so closely related to Baroque. As one of the earliest explorers of an unexplored art he seems at Hartwell to have furthered the idea that classical and romantic, usually kept apart, could be interwoven in a common landscape. This was perhaps the first stepping stone towards the conception of the present day plan: that reconstruction should be composed of *all* the strands of history, including those of to-day. The argument being that terrestrial space and time are thereby unified.

Ditchley Park: The enclosed garden elevation.

Lying in north Oxfordshire between Vanbrugh's two great mansions of Blenheim Palace and Heythrop, Ditchley was built between 1720 and 1724 and is considered the domestic masterpiece of James Gibbs, the architect of St. Martins-in-the-Fields, Trafalgar Square.

Ditchley Park: Plan c. 1727.

The house and approach avenues exist according to this plan, but the long terrace and enclosed garden to the south-west seem never to have been executed. Fashion in landscape changed during or immediately after the building of the house, classicism giving way to romanticism.

The house had replaced an earlier building in the vicinity and is well sited when seen from the Oxfordshire countryside to the south. But the north-west facade impinges on an awkward skew in the falling contours, and it was probably to rectify this that Gibbs proposed an unusually long terrace to act as a firm podium to his building. His conception of relation of architecture to landscape was authoritarian. (The present romantic park was not created until the last quarter of the eighteenth century).

Ditchley Park:
The plan of 1936.

The terms of reference from the owner were that the proposals for the new garden should take note of the Gibbs' plan, but should not reconstruct it purely as an historical exercise. Two centuries of civilisation were to modify the gardens just as they had the interior of the house itself. The new design is neo-classical, a reincarnation of both Alberti's and Wren's dictum that architecture should be built for eternity. In classical spirit the gardens are an extension of the architecture of the house and not a landscape in their own right. Ditchley is to-day the home of an Anglo-American Foundation, is virtually unchanged and will remain a testament to classical values in a world in constant change.

Note:
The plan of the garden in Grove Terrace is shown for comparison in scale just above the designer's initials.

111

The enclosed garden 1938. The parterre is now grass.

The enclosed garden 1938. The secret jets were to conceal bathers from the house.

The smaller enclosed garden 1978, which no longer exists.

The terrace from the south-east.

The terrace from the north-west.
The terminus of this view is a classical temple removed from the woods.

The landscape beyond the terrace.

This was made under the influence of Capability Brown some fifty years after the original Gibbs' plan, when the area appears to have been meadowland crossed by a rivulet. The terrain was difficult since the land fell *convex* rather than *concave* to the valley. The present unbalanced scene is skilfully based on a distant temple, but the illusion of a broad river without visible ends was destroyed when, soon after completion, the eastern half of the lake would not hold water. Unlike the integrated landscape of Hartwell, classicism and romanticism are kept severely apart.

Hartwell House as seen from the south-west. The view comprehends the significant phases of history which have been assembled in the modern plan on page 129. The medieval village lay beside the parish church(C) re-built in the eighteenth-century gothic revival.

Features are: A: eighteenth-century mansion B: Jacobean mansion C: parish church D: castellated tower E: site of eighteenth century bridge F: column of George II G: the Gibbs' pavilion H: equestrian statue of Frederick, Prince of Wales I: sculpture placed by Gibbs. The wavy late eighteenth-century paths and the royal crowns in yew commemorating the stay of Louis XVIII of France, are just visible. The circular nineteenth-century pool will be removed.

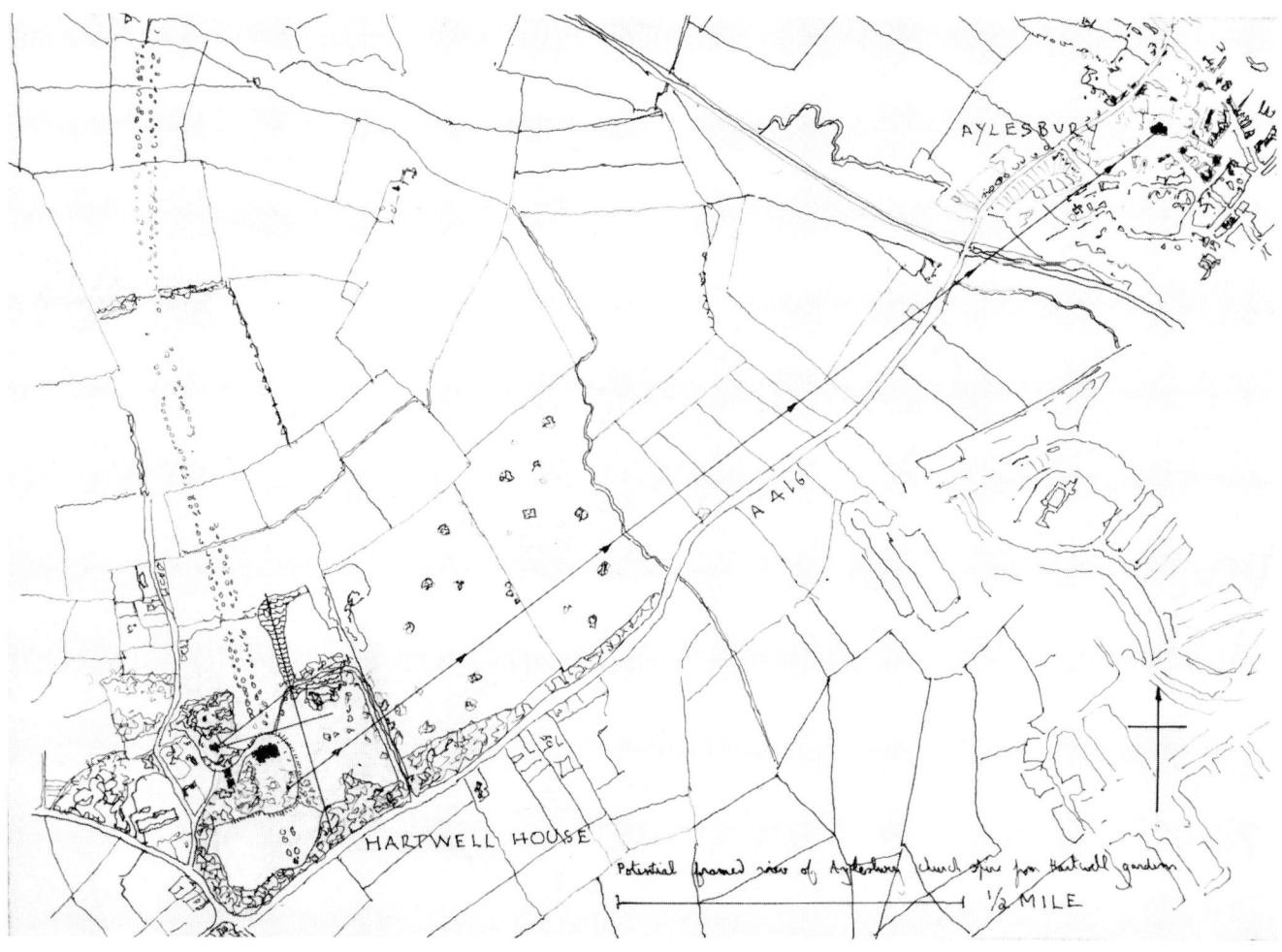

The first habitat was sited above the valley floor on land rising immediately west of the present house. It is said that a feudal tenant of King John derived his name and his home from a spring from which harts drank. The estate prospered. The great Jacobean mansion was built when the owner's heiress "gave her husband, Sir Thomas Lee, Bart. not only twenty-four children but also some of the most fertile land in the Vale of Aylesbury".

(Hartwell House, guide)

The map shows the triangulation of the romantic landscape round the mansion and the relation of park to Aylesbury church spire − prominent in the paintings by Balthasar Nebot (page 121) and one that, as indicated, can be isolated to-day from its modern context. The gentle "swing" of the field hedges in the vale has governed the shaping of the park, including the late 18th century entrance drive from the Aylesbury road.

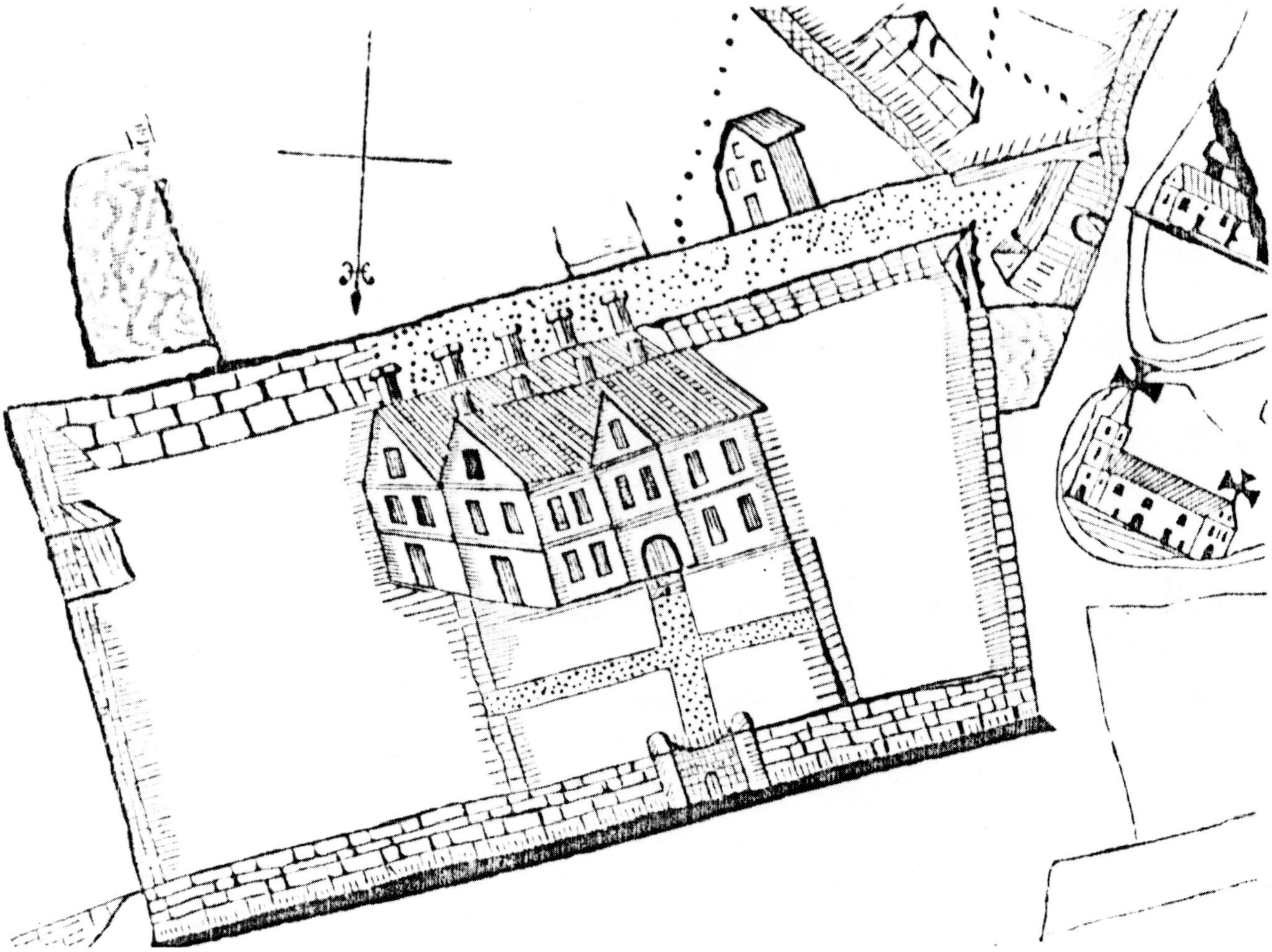

Early seventeenth century prints (a) and (b).

It is not easy to interpret this drawing (a) (top). Probably it was made by an enthusiastic layman interested in the new-fangled style of architecture emanating from Renaissance Italy rather than the traditional Jacobean actually built.

Together with a print of the existing front (b) however, it gives a clue as to the geometry with which a contemporary building was surrounded. The present Jacobean facade seems to have had the formal forecourt which was both practical and a splendid foreground to architecture.

Gibbs' pavilion

Painting by
Balthasar Nebot c. 1738.
View towards
Aylesbury.

James Gibbs was called to Hartwell shortly after 1730 presumably to study the
rebuilding of the mansion in a Palladian style, but in effect to become
preoccupied with ideas in landscape. As at Ditchley he conceived a grand
classical garden which, though seemingly never executed for the same reason,
laid the foundation of the romantic triangulated composition which exists
to-day. Sometime during these studies an itinerant Spanish painter, Balthasar
Nebot, was commissioned to make imaginative paintings of Gibbs' developing
ideas. In doing so he created a series of drawings whose scope is not only
without equal in the English history of gardens, but a remarkable insight into
the way garden classicism might have developed in this century had it not been
confronted and overwhelmed by romanticism.

Painting by
Balthasar Nebot c. 1738.
View towards
Gibbs' pavilion.

In these two views the Gibbs' pavilion, the north front of the house and the column exist to-day. As depicted, the design fitted the topography and, even more nobly than at Ditchley, overlooked the Vale of Aylesbury to the distant spire. The topiary here and in the other paintings is optimistic, and there is no conclusive evidence that the gardens were in fact executed.

This existing view from the bridge towards the Gibbs' pavilion parallels the
Nebot painting (page 121) showing how the formal gardens would have fitted
the terrain. The house is out of sight to the right.

View of Henry Keene's classic facade of 1759, with the brick path as a reminder of the Picturesque style shown in the print on page 126.

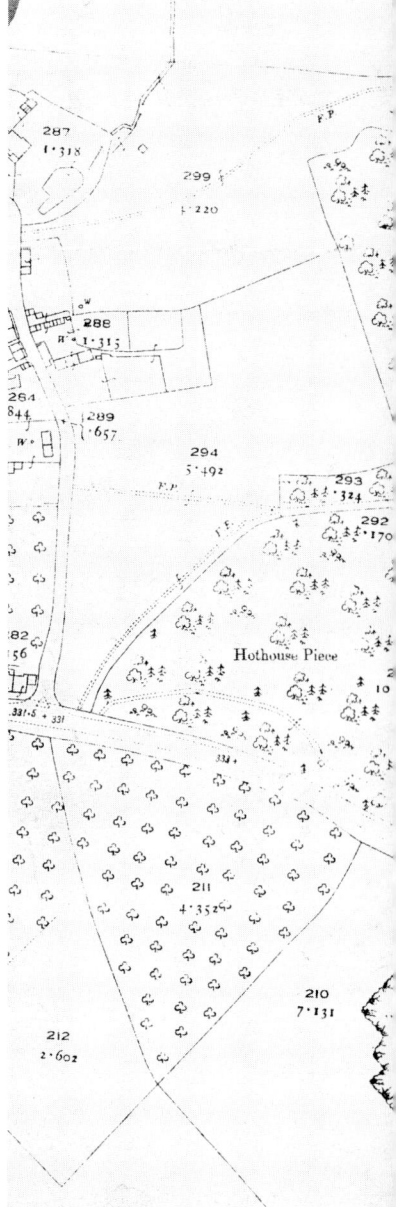

Plan dated 1777.

This is the first known authentic plan of the estate. The form was transitional and short lived. There is a new drive from a lodge on the Aylesbury road so disposed in its visual design of approach that the landscape composition of house and stables, and possibly the tower of the church in between, could be appreciated in their changing relationships. This is a conception of the kind furthered at that time by Humphry Repton, necessitating a change of entrance to the house from north to south. Probably the sharp rise from

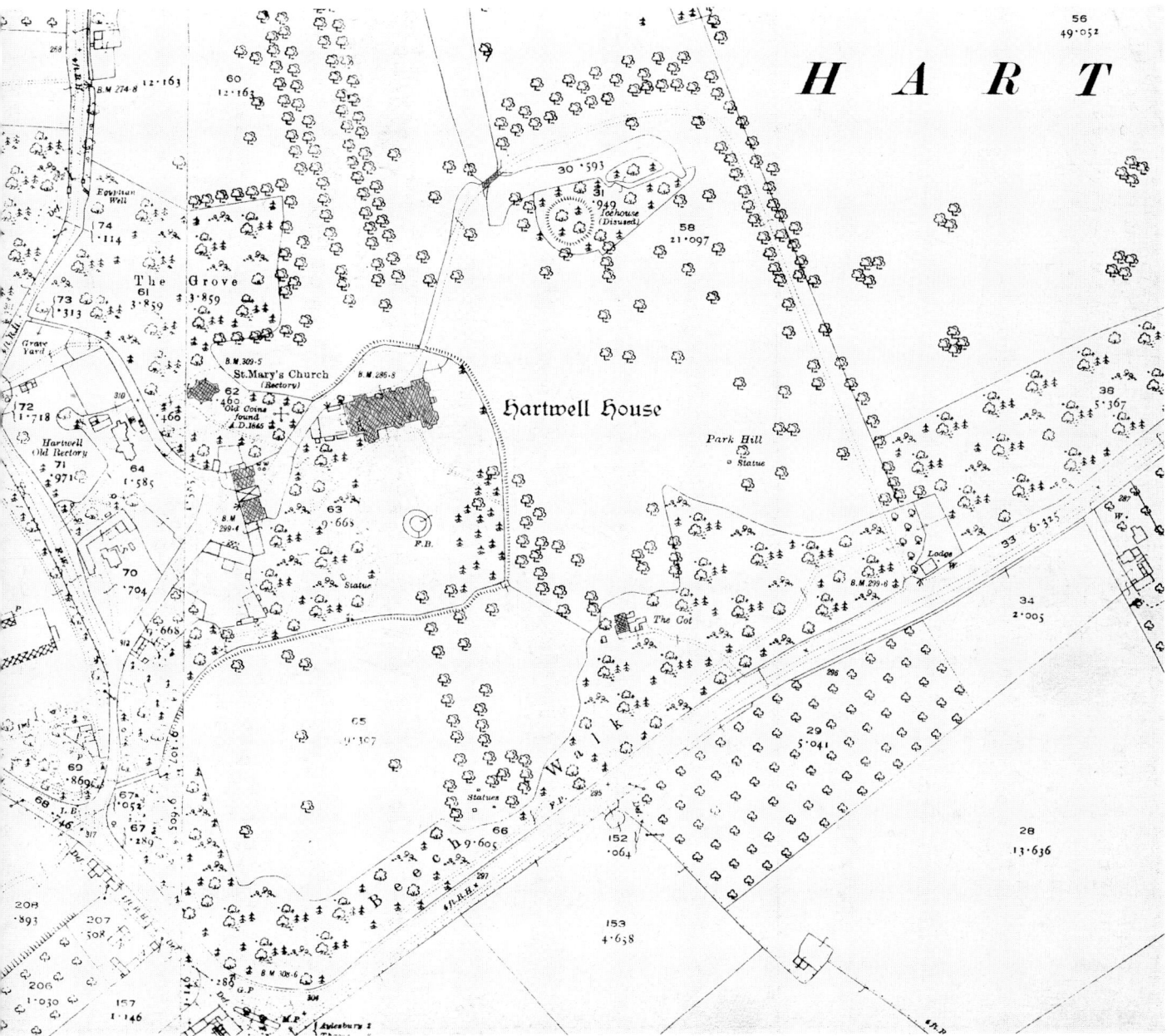

H A R T

Ordinary Survey
of site as existing.

forecourt to stables proved impracticable. The Gibbs pavilion is shown centred on the present elongated lake, but there is no bridge. It was the placing of this bridge three years later, to serve what became the main approach, that finally co-ordinated the romantic design. Directed towards the church and axial with the pavilion it was finally to form the third element that linked two objects or ideas in space. A comparison of the maps of 1777 and the modern ordnance show the developments that took place in the following two centuries.

The north facade is Jacobean; the south and east facades are mid 18th century classical by Henry Keene, who also built the gothic revival church and located the bridge (built by James Wyatt 1780 and later replaced). The foliage and winding paths about the house were probably made about 1795 under the influence of the poet William Mason. The great avenue to the north (out of sight in the entrance view) was planted 1820-1830. Incidentals included the two royal crowns (c.1807). The observatory, being built soon after 1827 and demolished soon after 1860, takes no part in this creative history. The half century between 1777 and 1827 admirably reflects the confusion of landscape ideas prevalent in the country as a whole.

The south elevation from a print post 1827.

Within the romantic movement there was a fundamental and loquacious split between the followers of the "shaven lawns" of Capability Brown and those of the picturesques, headed by Uvedale Price, Payne Knight and others including Mason who had designed the gardens of the neighbouring Nuneham Courtney. The split epitomised the dual personality of primeval man himself: man the *Hunter* (aggressive) and man the *Forester* (peaceloving). Across this confusion in the form of an avenue stretched the geometry of man the *Settler* (the rational).

The east and north
elevations from a
print post 1827,
showing the entrance.

It is probable that William Mason's book on gardens influenced
J. C. Loudon's development of "the gardenesque" style of design; wavy paths
and wild planting were human and tender rather than heroic at Hartwell.
Except for the circular pool (with its Gibbs "terms" moved here from the
pavilion), occasional planting of trees and shrubs, and the yew screen
extending from the north east corner of the house, there has been little
change in the last century and a half. There is no reflection of the classical
High Renaissance of the mid-nineteenth century, nor of the work of Gertrude
Jekyll, Edwin Lutyens, and the neo-georgian revival generally.

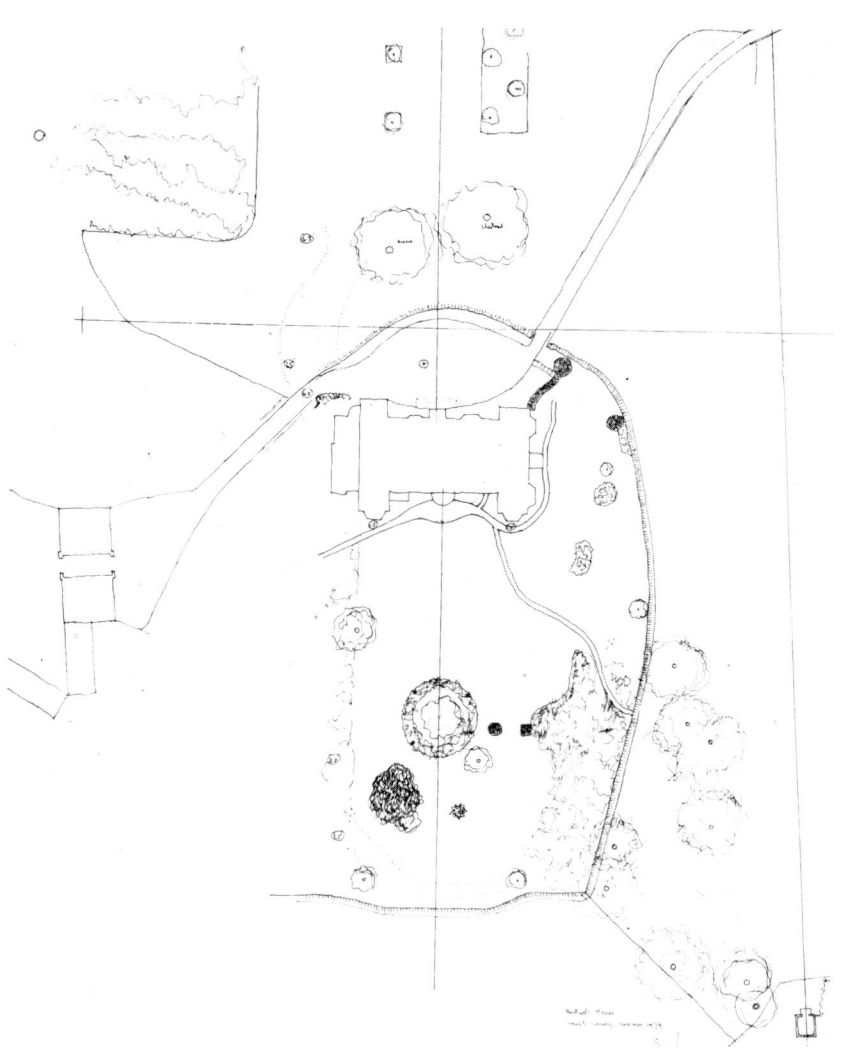

Plan proposed 17.8.79. ▶

Sketch Survey 1978.

The plan is intended to reveal the essence of landscape history and adapt it to modern needs. It is in this respect, therefore, a recreation rather than an original design. The inessential in history has been eliminated. The essential is the classical geometry (from Jacobean to Renaissance) which dominates; the heroic romantic landscape that interweaves with it; and the tender "gardenesque" (if the wavy paths can be so-called) that complete the composition. To adapt itself to the car, the forecourt has been extended to add dignity to what is still a noble facade and to allow parking only on exceptionable occasions. A new car park for daily use is an extended "after"-court to the eighteenth century stables. A sun terrace has been formed south of the house. The equestrian statue of Frederic has been opened to view from the stables entrance (as apparently shown in the 1777 plan); the Gibbs pavilion has been dignified by clipped hedges to frame a potentially beautiful picture of bridge and lake beyond; a view of Aylesbury church spire opened up, in sympathy with the Nebot paintings; and clear views within the triangulation restored.

This plan is intended to be like a tapestry woven of once antagonistic threads, now reconciled and each part of a unified whole, whose 'time' is the present.

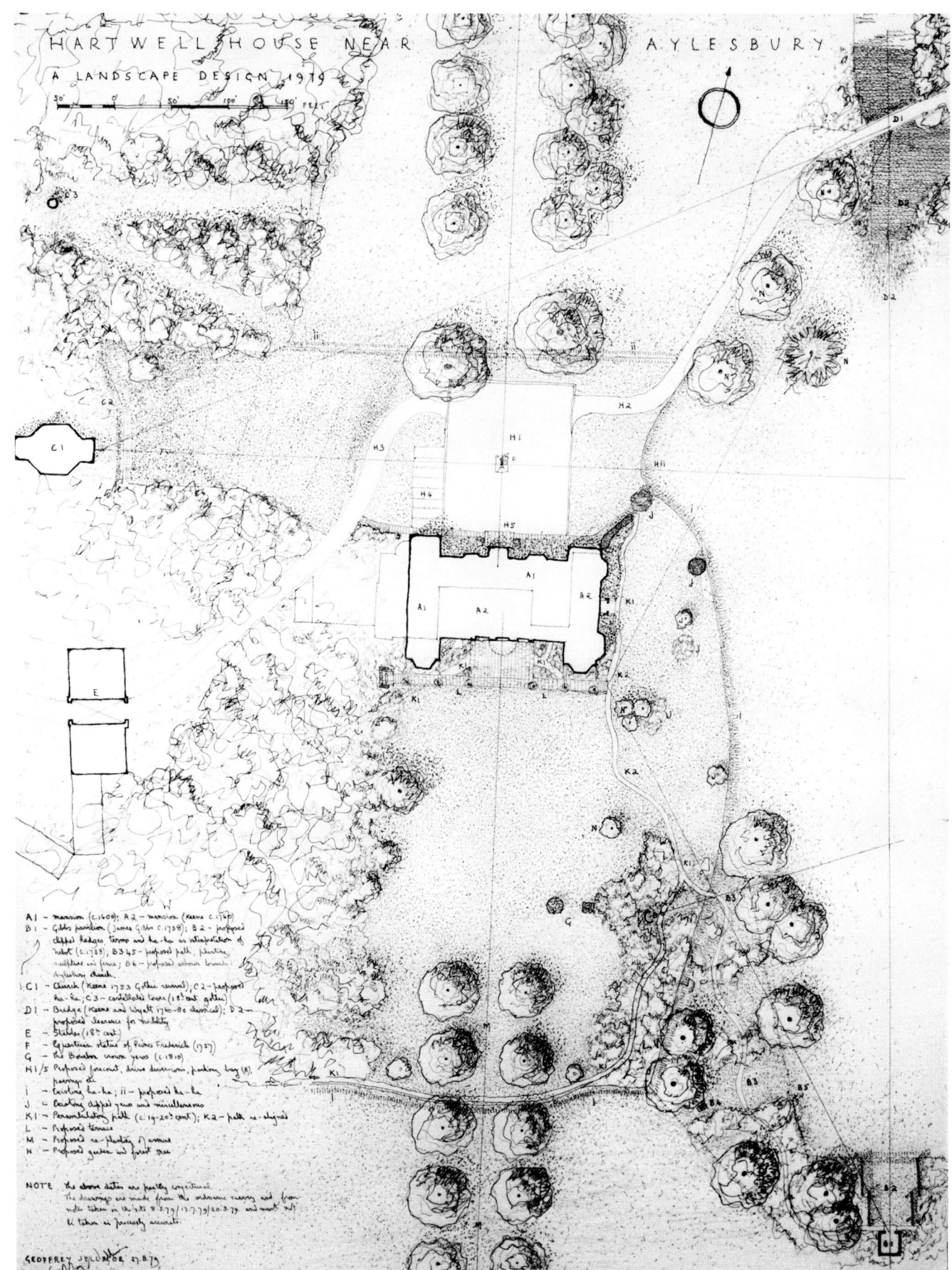

HARTWELL HOUSE NEAR · AYLESBURY

A LANDSCAPE DESIGN 1979

50'   0'   50'   100'   150 FEET

A1 – mansion (c.1600); A2 – mansion (Keene c.1760)
B1 – Gibbs pavilion (James Gibbs c.1738); B2 – proposed
    clipped hedges, terrace and ha-ha as interpretation of
    tablet (c.1738), B3 & 5 – proposed path, planting,
    sculpture and fence; B6 – proposed avenue towards
    Aylesbury church
C1 – Church (Keene 1753 Gothic revival); C2 – proposed
    ha-ha; C3 – castellated tower (18th cent gothic)
D1 – Bridge (Keene and Wyatt 1760–80 classical); D2 –
    proposed licensee for building
E – Stables (18th cent)
F – Equestrian statue of Prince Frederick (1757)
G – the Bandon crown yews (c.1810)
H1/5 Proposed forecourt, drive diversion, parking bay (8),
    passings etc
I – Existing ha-ha; ii – proposed ha-ha
J – Existing clipped yews and miscellaneous
K1 – Perambulation path (c.19–20th cent); K2 – path re-aligned
L – Proposed terrace
M – Proposed re-planting of avenue
N – Proposed garden and forest tree

NOTE the above dates are partly conjectural
    the drawings are made from the ordnance survey and from
    notes taken on the site 8.2.79/12.7.79/20.8.79 and must not
    be taken as precisely accurate

GEOFFREY JELLICOE 27.8.79

129

Blue Circle Hope Cement Works – DERBYSHIRE

Commission: 1943-79

While Hartwell can be considered a simple study in terrestrial time/space, the industrial landscape in progress at Hope is concerned with man's relation to the cosmos itself. A fifty year plan, the first of its kind in England, was commissioned in 1943; it assumed a fixed life for the works and its principles were orthodox and those accepted at the time. Thirty-six years later a progress report seemed to reveal that an entirely new landscape art form might be evolving, one parallel to those explored by the artists since the beginning of the century.

As a metaphysical introduction to a physical comparison of the two plans, the following is taken from the appendix of the 1979 report:

"Depending upon whom you are, the works at Hope can register as an unwelcome intrusion into a National Park or as a welcome symbol of prosperity for the neighbourhood.

Neither of these associations of ideas, however, have any bearing on whether the industrial landscape envisaged for 1993 is or is not a new art form. Certainly none of the components – works and quarries – can be considered individually to be so: but can they in the conglomerate with a little judicious encouragement? Does the modest slotting in of a high terrace into a grove of trees, whose shape was dictated centuries ago, make all this difference?

The works are splendid as complex geometry drawing upon the laws of the universe, but their design is inhuman and scientific rather than architectural. The breath-taking limestone quarry, governed by the unpredictable qualities of the stone and the legal restrictions of height that control the terrace, is an awe-inspiring void certainly not designed for aesthetics.

The shale quarries at the present moment are less dramatic except for their size, but it is impossible to foretell their future.

This landscape, if it really were an art, illustrates the aesthetic of John Dewey, recognised by Bertrand Russell and others as the greatest American philosopher of the first half of the twentieth century.

The way of thought is new to the western world and is paralleled by action painting, particularly of Jackson Pollock. Dewey maintained art was not merely the finished object, but the whole experience of creation. He believed that art was a unity of time and space, an experience that should have a beginning and a consummation. He conceived art, therefore, as a series of experiences, which by analogy he turned into landscape:

'In such experiences, every successive part flows freely, without seam and without unfilled blanks, into what ensues. At the same time there is no sacrifice of the self-identity of the parts. A river, as distinct from a pool, flows. But its successive portions are greater than exist in the homogeneous portions of a pond. In an experience, flow is from something to something. As one part carries on what went before, each gains distinction in itself.

The enduring whole is diversified by successive phases that are an emphasis of its varied colours.'

From which it can be deduced that the 1943 conception of a fifty year plan was classical and finite, whereas the present revision accepts that the art (action-landscape) lies in the experience of evolution as much as in the end, even if an end (or "enduring whole") were conceivable".

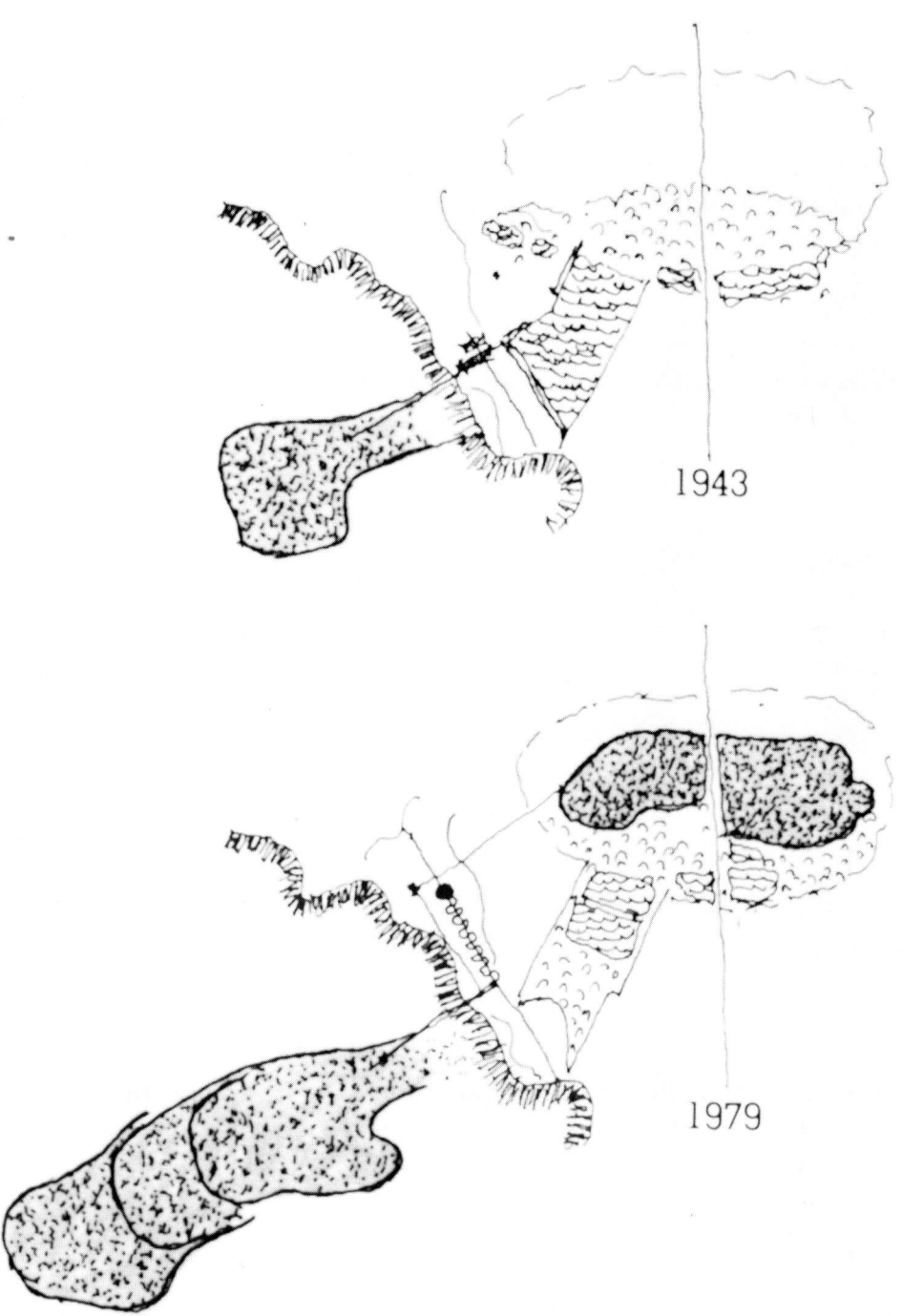

1943

1979

Diagrams enlarged from thumb-nail sketches in the 1979 Report to illustrate the change of planning theory that took place between 1943 and 1979. The first plan (page 134) assumed finality after fifty years and its eventual form to be classical and static. Thirty-six years later the second plan (page 141) accepted that classicism could play only a minor part in the fluid and constantly growing organism that was creating its own land forms.

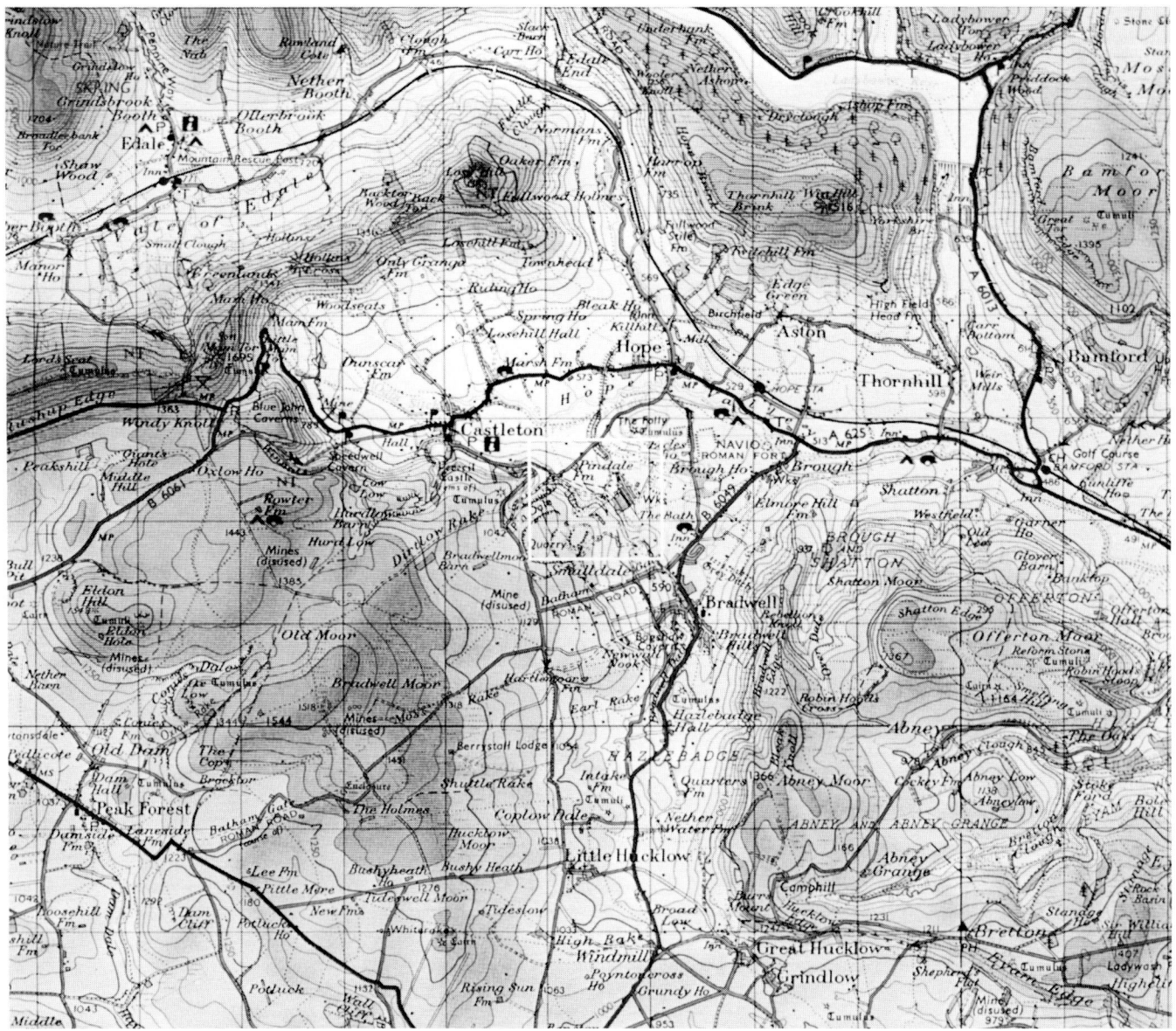

Map showing location among the mountains in 1929.

Attracted here by the raw materials and easy transport to markets, Earle's Cement Works (as they were then called) were established in 1929 in the centre of what is now the Peak District National Park in Derbyshire. They are equidistant from the villages of Castleton, Hope, Brough and Bradwell and they lie opposite to Win Hill of which Ebenezer Elliott (1781-1849) wrote:

King of the Peak! Win Hill! thou throned and crowned
That reign'st o'er many a stream and many a vale
Star-loved, and meteor sought, and tempest found!
Proud centre of the mountain circle, hail!
The might of man may triumph or may fail
But, Eldest Brother of the Air and Light,
Firm shall thou stand when Demi-gods turn pale!
For thou, ere Science dawned on Reasons' night
Wast, and will be when mind shall rule all other might.

But this may not be so.

The works in 1943 looking south-west across the playing fields towards the lime quarries.

An appreciation of the site from the Report of 1943:

The landscape consists in bare hills and between them a fertile valley. The beauty of the scene lies in the contrast of the two, the timelessness of the one and the vitality and changefulness of the other. It is essential to retain in mind these two associations of ideas.

The works lie at the foot of the hills, the quarries above, and the exposed clay pits in the valley. The waste from the quarries has been used to form a platform on the hillside. The stone is carried down the slopes through a visible surface tunnel, but the clay is pumped underground through invisible pipes. The buildings themselves are well and compactly grouped, and, on the side towards the valley, lie beside green playing fields.

The conflict of ideas may be summarised as follows:
a) the quarries and the platform disturb the contours, denote change, and destroy the sense of loneliness
b) the clay excavations have created a derelict area in the midst of fertility
c) the buildings themselves denote a manufacturing rather than an agricultural industry.

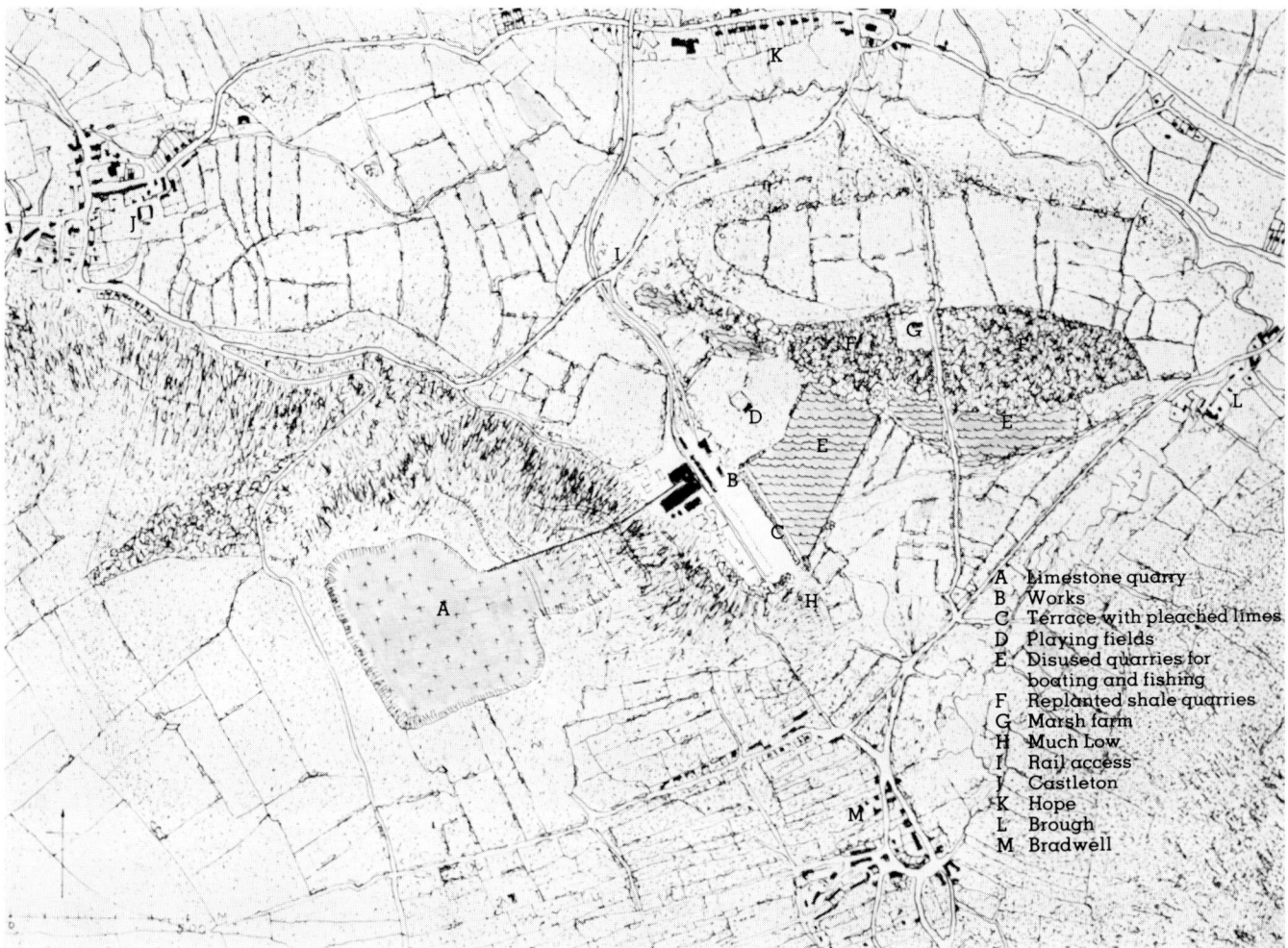

The fifty-year landscape plan 1943-93.

Fourteen years after the establishment of the works in 1929, the limestone quarries consisted in a modest excavation carved out of the hillside.

In the valleys were water-filled shale quarries (which were to be increased) and the beginnings of unsightly dry shale excavations on the adjoining slopes. The plan of 1943 was an imaginary composition of fifty years ahead, based on known fact and necessary assumptions, to the fulfilment of which all interim development would be directed.

By the end of the century the works would be disbanded and the site made over to public recreation. The main points were:

1) The natural silhouette of the surrounding hills must be retained.

2) The mouth of the expanding limestone quarry should be kept to the minimum and the adjoining escarpment restored to the original.

3) The water quarries would be extended to form pleasure lakes, the untidy marshalling yards being concealed by a terrace of pleached limes.

4) Tree planting to be continued throughout the whole period, especially on the visible shale quarries; and every endeavour made to encourage the return of wild life.

The plan is a finite composition, a free rendering of the principles of classical garden design.

The model, showing the classical composition with the romantic.

The following are extracts from the 1943 Report accompanying the plan itself:

1) "Although the design was first intended to be one of amelioration of existing conditions, it is hoped it may suggest that industry could in fact become an asset in the countryside.

   The landscape plan should normally be prepared simultaneously with, and not after the industrial plan: in the future the two plans should be one and the same.

6) The impact of such an industry upon an agricultural community is a sociological study that is in itself extremely interesting. The Report of the Committee on Land Utilisation in Rural Areas has made a preliminary survey of the problem, and this plan illustrates some of the arguments. Integration between new-comers and existing inhabitants appears essential if both are to have the full benefits of what each can give. This suggests that while the villages can give the required facilities for mixing in winter, the Works can supply outdoor facilities beyond the means of any village community. These will include, cricket, bowls, golf, boating, bathing and fishing, and in addition, football in winter. For the factory worker particularly, it is hoped that the informal lake and surrounding scenery will give him a perception of nature quicker and more deeply than would a normal agricultural landscape".

The assumptions of future production and growth made in 1943 were too modest as regards both demand and methods of manufacture. The increased demand was reflected in a call on the quarries far beyond the original calculations. The effect on the buildings themselves of a change in technique from a wet to dry process was more dramatic. This illustration shows them after twenty five years progress of the plan — a fundamental change symbolised by the metamorphosis of two chimneys into one.

The four main points of the original plan, however remained as guidelines. The landscape consultant — Mrs. Sheila Haywood, originally an assistant on the 1943 plan and consultant throughout the thirty-six years, writes particularly of the progress of ecology:

"The planting of trees and shrubs at Hope has been a continuous programme since the inception of the original landscape plan. Linked with planting has gone careful ground shaping, and the constructive use of wastes, to provide screening where necessary, and to link with existing ground. Nowhere has this been more important than in the bankings leading up to the great limestone quarry. Early planting concentrated upon the works area, and to-day the approach to the works itself, the railway line,

The works in 1968.

and the south-western margins of the playing fields are linked by belts of mature trees: Norway maple, poplar, ash and mountain ash, wild cherry and many others. These, underplanted by such shrubs as dogwood, snowberry, guelder rose and the wild privet for ground level screening, provided country character right up to the reception area itself. Here, by contrast an older and more formal lay-out has been retained as a link with the earliest days of the Works. A considerable achievement has been the retention, unharmed, of large established trees throughout major extensions to the works, in close proximity to the new buildings. The lakes to-day are fringed with birch and willow, their northern shores closely wooded, with natural regeneration taking over from man's handiwork, with a more open planting on the south-west. Meanwhile, as the designer envisaged, considerable bird life has come to the valley, and in particular to the lakes".

The second metamorphosis of the structure into that of the present day. "Geometry, in particular, is a Greek invention without which modern science would have been impossible".

Bertrand Russell in *A History of Western Philosophy*

View from the west of works and landscape, 1979.

To the overriding unpredictability of market forces and technical invention has been added that of the raw material. Thus its unsuitability as a shale quarry prevented the completion of the formal pleasure lake; vast extra shale quarries were opened on the adjoining hillside; and the limestone quarries far exceeded in size and fluidity of form any original calculation.

Nevertheless, despite the changes in both quarries and buildings the two essential points in the original plan had been retained; that the works should be contained within the silhouette of the hills and the escarpment preserved, and that there should be continuous tree planting.

An internal explosion from the original plan had been inevitable, and from it had emerged a conception of space that could be recognised as being far grander than the original. The only adjustment proposed for this dramatic

140

A Limestone quarry
B Works
C Platform
D Playing fields
E Disused shale quarries
   (fishing lakes, etc)
F Replanted shale quarries
F1 Shale quarries in use
G Marsh Farm
H Much Low
I Rail access
J Castleton
K Hope
L Brough
M Bradwell

The plan of 1943-93 as reassessed in 1979.

self-creating landscape was the re-shaping of the southern platform now being made out of waste (c).

This would complete the geometry at the centre and relate it to the countryside.

Two factors set the Hope landscape apart from any experience of humanism. It is monstrous in size and in its relation to the humans who attend upon it, and like a monster it is in constant growth with a power that will only be seriously tested when it meets the limits of its cage many decades ahead. Is or is not this extraordinary and deeply impressive man-created landscape a work of art? It exactly expresses the philosophy of flux of John Dewey, but does it relate to the twentieth century abstract painters in their exploration into space/time?

141

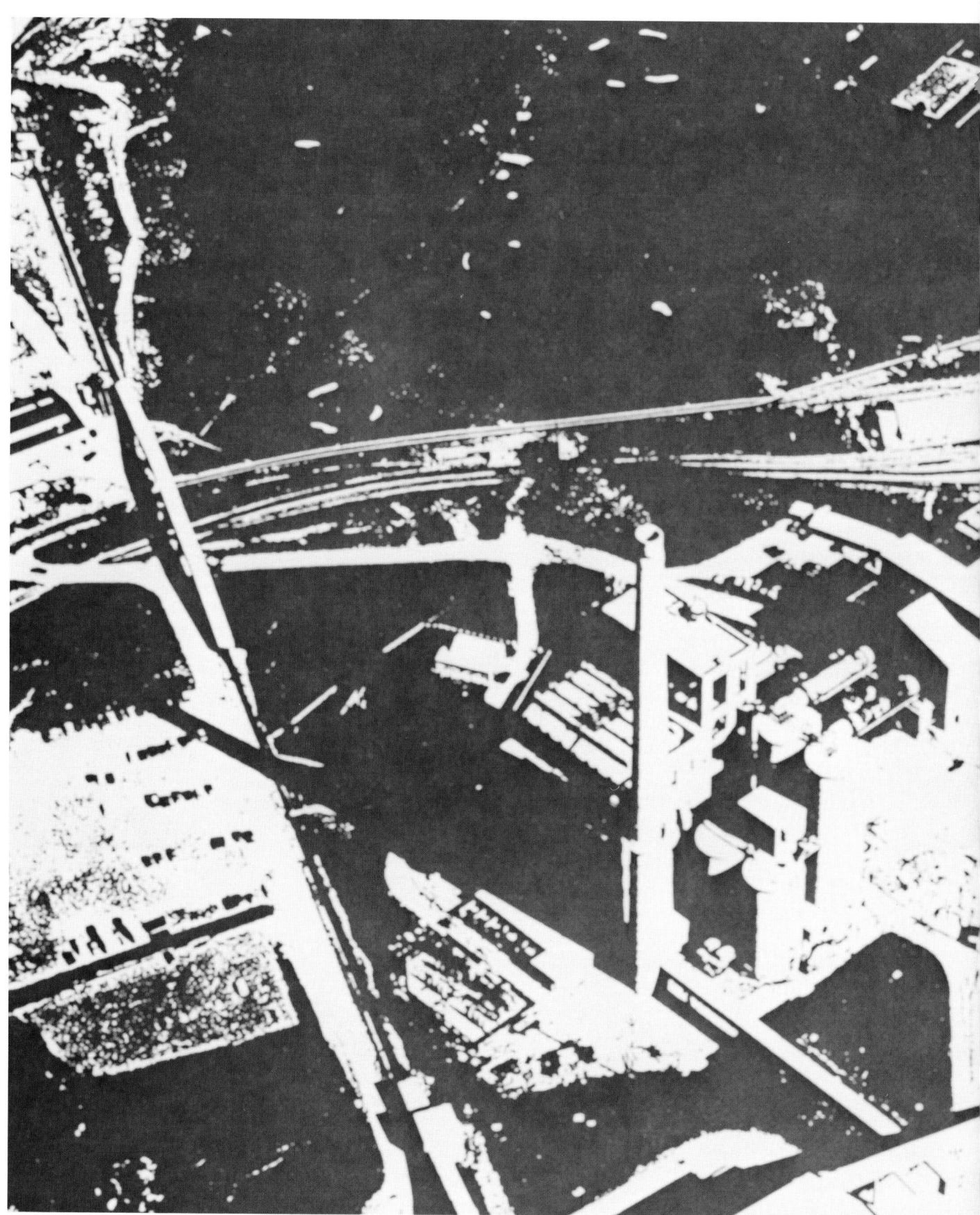

Action-landscape: aerial view of the works 1979.

143

Jackson Pollock: Painting, 1952

This self-evolving art, if it is an art, seems to parallel the action painting of abstract expressionism.

The leading exponent, Jackson Pollock, declared that the canvas rather than himself took charge of a painting.

H.H. Aranson writes in *A History of Modern Art*:

"Aside from their intrinsic quality, Pollock's drip paintings contributed other elements that changed the course of modern painting. There was, first, the concept of the overall painting, seemingly without beginning or end, extending to the very limits of the canvas and implying an extension even beyond. This, together with the large scale of the works, introduced another concept — that of wall painting different from the tradition of easel painting, even as it existed in cubism and geometric abstraction. This was the final break from the Renaissance idea of painting detached from spectator, to be looked at as a self-contained unit.

The painting became an environment, an ensemble, which encompassed the spectator, surrounding him on all sides. The feeling of absorption or participation is heightened by the ambiguity of the picture space. The colours and lines, although never puncturing deep perspective holes in the surface, still create an illusion of continuous movement, a billowing, a surging back and forth, within a limited depth."

The scene is tranquil enough, because the machine is guided, groomed and restrained.

But what of the future?

In the same period ahead of the 250 years since Elliott wrote his poem, the expanding monster could have consumed quantity-wise the whole of the hills in this view, with Win Hill (out of the picture to the right) thrown in for good measure. Can humanist values survive in such a whirl as this portends?

"Can we, as did the simpler past civilisations, turn scientific data into abstract thought and art, thus to sustain and identify ourselves as humans and not as animals in this extraordinary continuum?"

Landscape of Man: Epilogue

"King of the Peak! Win Hill! thou throned and crowned
That reign'st o'er many a stream and many a vale!
Star-loved, and meteor-sought, and tempest-found!
Proud centre of the mountain circle, hail!
The might of man may triumph or may fail,
But, Eldest Brother of the Air and Light,
Firm shall thou stand when Demi-gods turn pale!
For thou, ere Science dawned on Reason's night
Wast, and will be when mind shall rule all other might."

Ebenezer Elliott, 1781-1849.

View across Castleton from Holdins Cross.

Lecture IV

TOWARDS A LANDSCAPE OF HUMANISM

The drawings for Sutton Place, Guildford.

Introduction

Sutton Place is now administered by a Trust, but the drawings shown in this lecture were prepared for, and inspired by, an individual. Stanley Seeger recognised that history is a continuum of the past, present and future, and that an objective in landscape design is not to smother history, but to build on it. The landscape at Sutton Place is of the mind as well as the eye: a study in humanism emanating from the interior of an historic mansion enriched with modern art.

Apart from the loss of the gatehouse in the eighteenth century, the external appearance of the mansion itself has remained virtually constant since 1522, when it was built for Richard Weston in a style transitional between medieval and Renaissance. While the architecture has remained static, the landscape over the four and a half centuries has created and recreated itself in three distinct phases, each phase being an expression of the culture of the time. First came the kitchen gardens with their protective walls and the authoritarian avenue approach, the whole set in a hunting park. The present classical ethos of place was decisively established at this time, strong enough (as history records) to eject Capability Brown when he proposed the destruction of the avenue and its replacement by the then fashionable Brownian landscape.

The second phase came about at the turn of the present century. The historic ethos of place was recognised, accepted and developed. The classical axiality was continued on the south side by an avenue of yews, while a yew-defined terrace created a commanding cross axis. The geometry upon which the third or present phase was to be based was then complete in all but a true balance about the house (the idea of the spectacular rectangle of daffodils planted at that time may have been a throw-back, conscious or unconscious, to the Field of the Cloth of Gold, which Weston attended as a statesman of Henry VIII. The feeling of this period sentimentalised a golden age of chivalry).

The third or present phase has turned for its structure to the period in Italian history known as Mannerism, and particularly to an individual garden, the Villa Gamberaia at Settignano. From this source and from Weston's own Sutton Place has evolved the philosophy of a particular purpose of landscape design in the modern world. While Sutton Place provided an unsophisticated ethos of place, Gamberaia provided the visionary concept that within a framework of rational order it is possible (and desirable) to include those mysterious aspects of the mind that are creations of the subconscious. First, these two sources together constitute a statement of classical values whose recognition seems to become the more imperative the faster we move into the unknown. Secondly, interwoven with the reasoned geometry of classicism, and humanising it, are the unreasoned fantasia of the subconscious, released in all their fun, oddity and awesomeness. It would seem that to project into the environment the *whole* and not merely part of the mind of man, individual or collective, is the highest objective in the creation of landscape as an art.

Nearly two years after the plans were made and work had commenced, there emerged the concept of a grand allegory that had unconsciously directed the composition. This allegory is one of *Creation* (the lake landscape), *Life* (the gardens) and *Aspiration* (the Nicholson Wall). It clearly derives from the allegory concealed in the Kennedy Memorial (page 86) and like all allegories, is intended to lift the spirit for a brief period out of the present. When Ben Nicholson was asked the meaning of his Wall, he replied, "How should *I* know?" (page 194)

Sutton Place Surrey.

Sutton Place – GUILDFORD

Early print showing the gatehouse before its removal in the eighteenth century. Unlike the existing kitchen garden walls there are no signs that those of a pleasure garden on the east were ever built.

Eighteenth century plan of estate before demolition of the gatehouse. A double avenue is indicated, but unlike the present avenue, which frames the whole facade, the earlier avenue was narrowed to concentrate on the gatehouse tower.

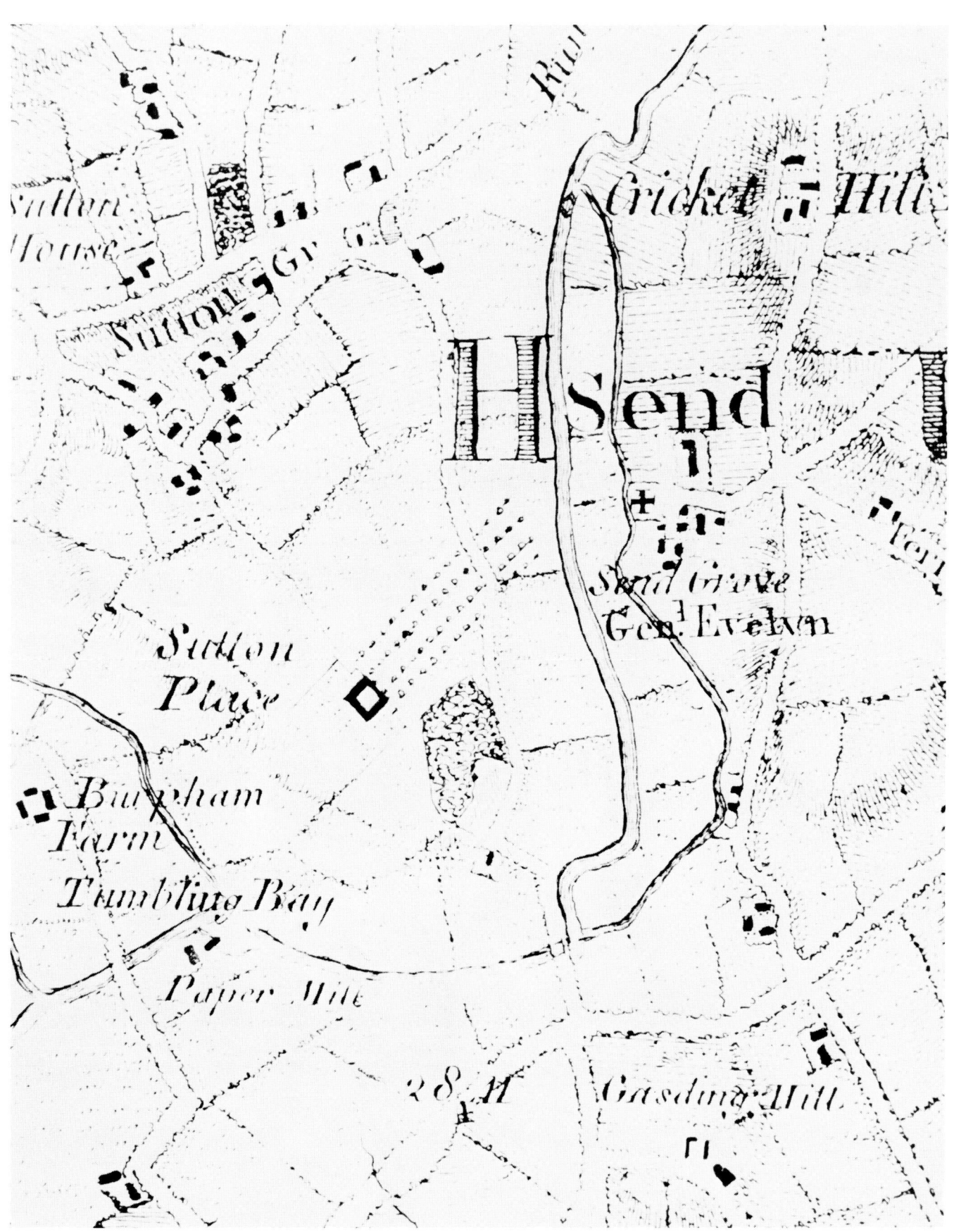

Sutton
House

Sutton Gr.

Cricket Hill

H Send

Sutton
Place

Send Grove
Genl Evelyn

Burpham
Farm

Tumbling Bay

Paper Mill

28 M

Gasding Hill

151

Sutton Place

This air view of the gardens from the south taken before the present works, shows the unaltered sixteenth century house set in early twentieth century gardens in which Gertrude Jekyll was involved.

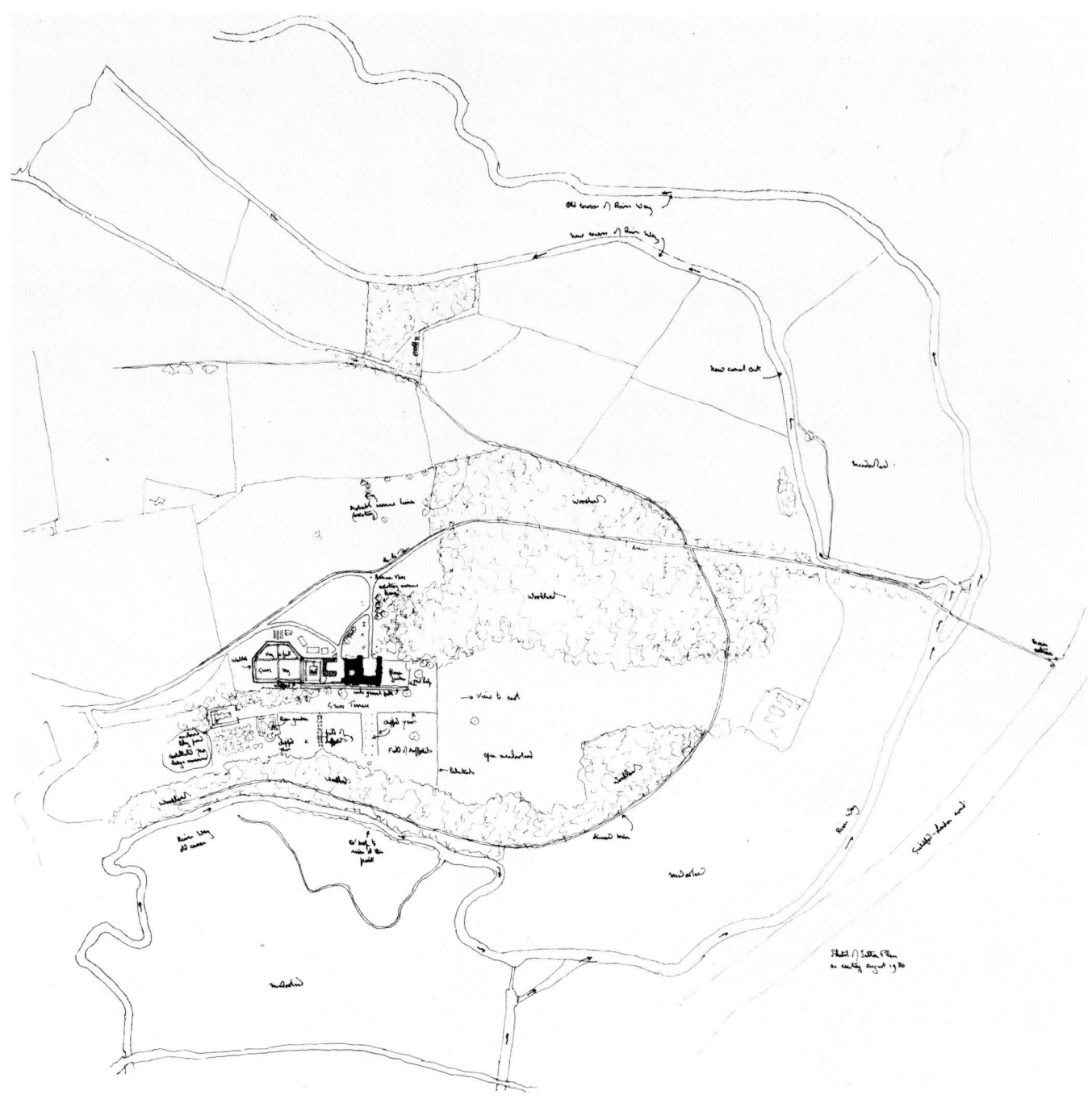

Sketch survey of Sutton Place as existing August 1980.

The rough survey reveals the relation of mansion to terrain and especially to the windings of the river Wey (the canalised by-pass is eighteenth century). The remnants of the long original "closed" avenue can be seen. Although unbalanced about the central axis, the historic classical structure of the domestic landscape is clear.

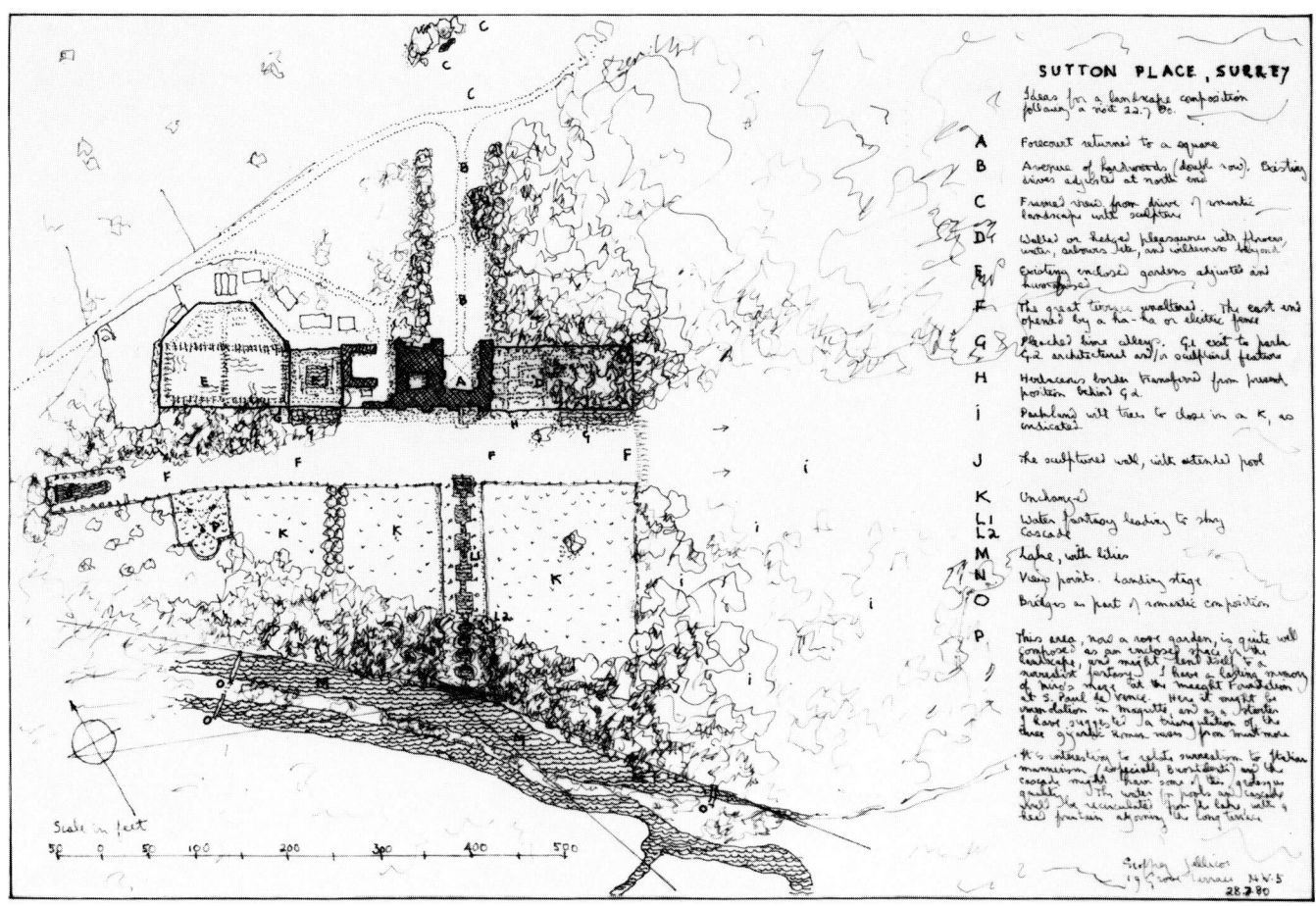

The first sketch made after a one-day visit to Sutton Place in July 1980, and upon which was made the decision to proceed. Except for the transfer of the lake there has been no major change in the composition.

Sutton Place

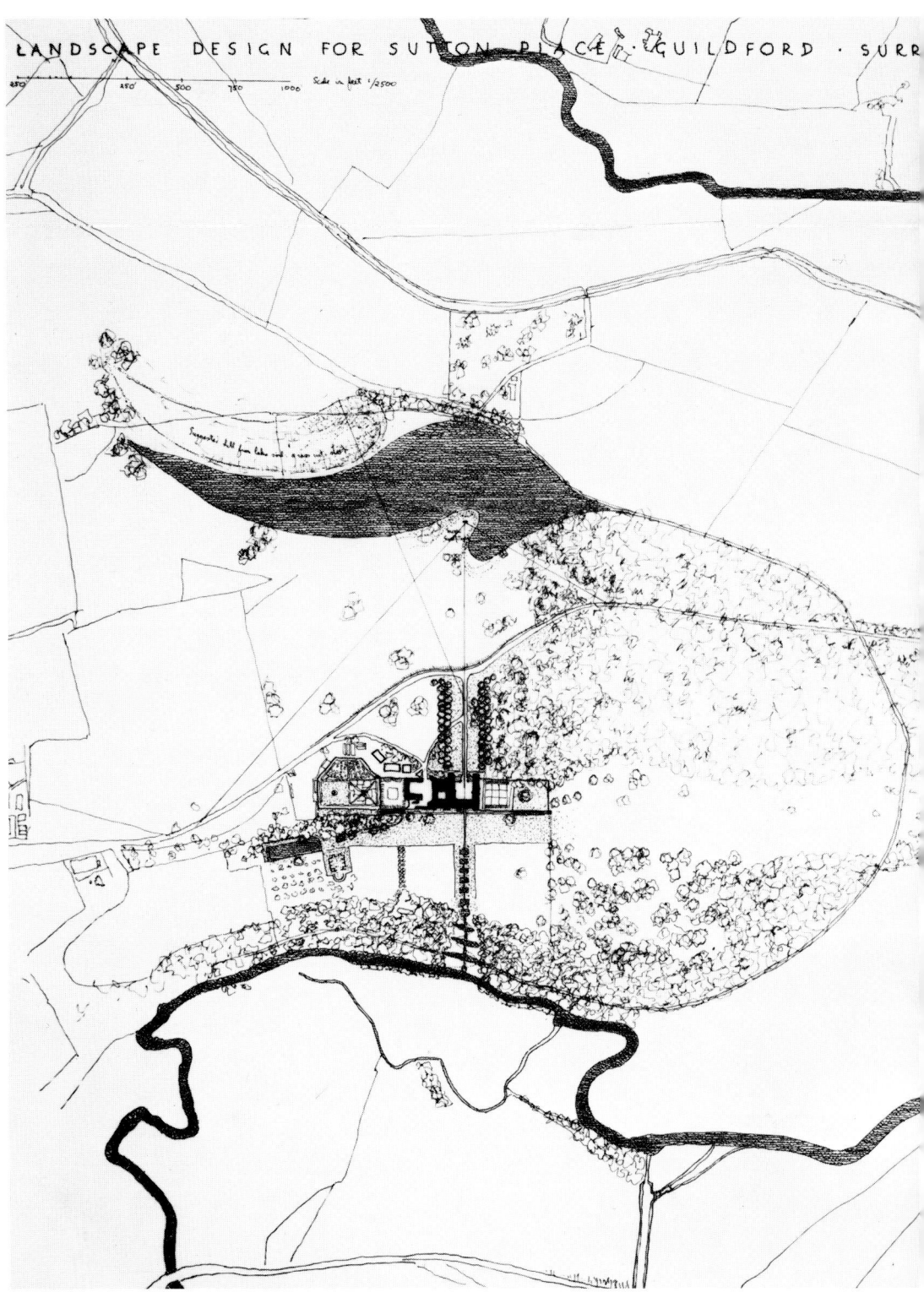

The concept developed by September 1980. The lake has been transferred to the north; the drawing emphasises its relation to the primeval rather than the artificial course of the river Wey.
At the right: the remnants of the traditional "closed" avenue are seen within the newly planted fifty trees commemorating the fiftieth birthday of the owner.

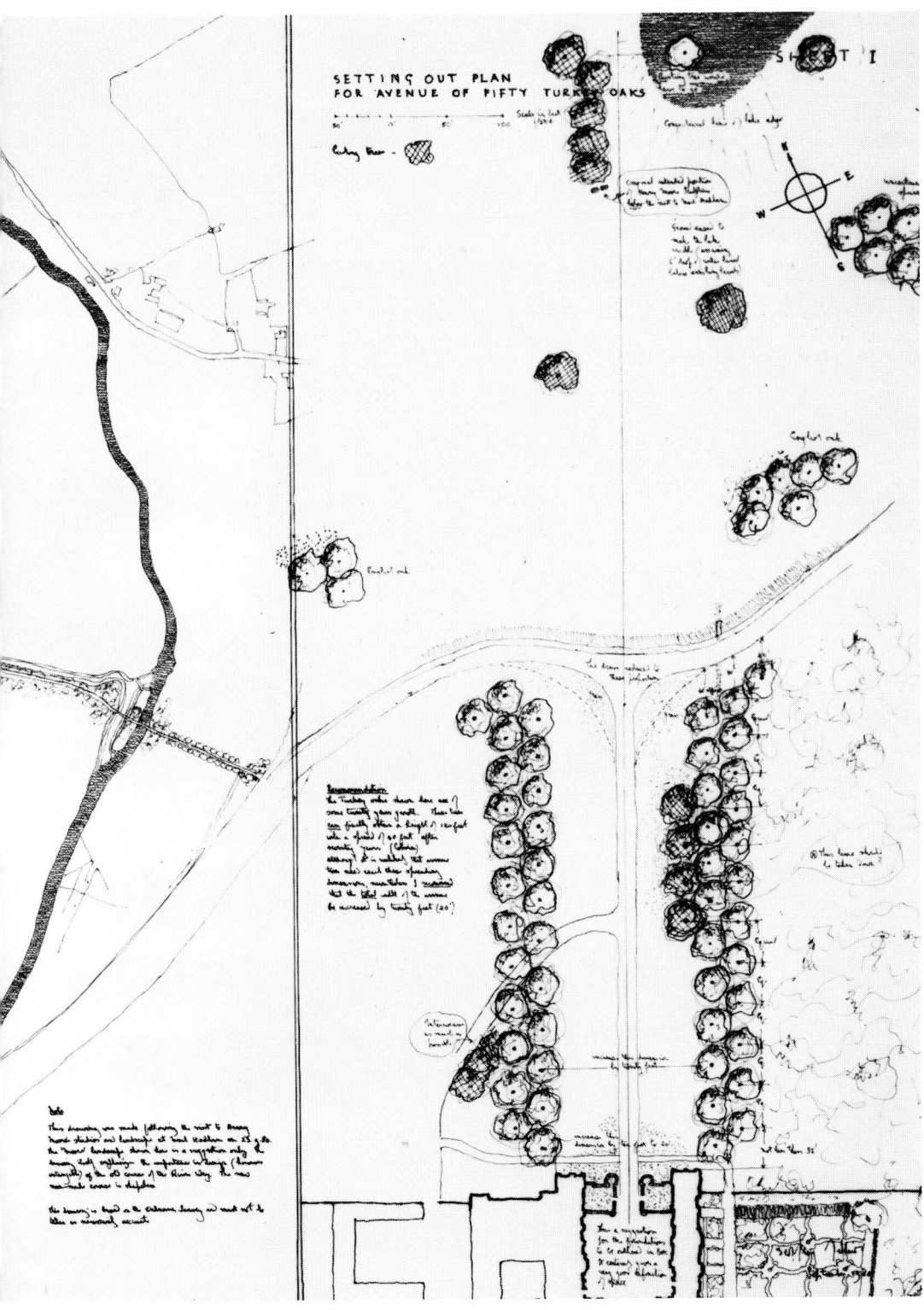

Introduction to an Ecological Study

prepared by Marian Thompson ALI. January - April 1981.

The terms of reference given were "To study the present ecology of the area between the walled gardens and the fringe farmland, and present scientific proposals as a basis of landscape art".

Ecology is the body of knowledge concerning nature's economy, its study, the investigation of the total relations of plants and animals in their environment. Nature strives for balance; past and present human activity have profound effects on this natural balance. This understanding and the great potential for ecological diversification and enrichment which the new design brings to the estate, were the motives for commissioning this study. An estate with woodlands, wild shrubs, grassland, gardens and water is naturally rich in wildlife. To look only at the areas directly affected by the design would be to deny the important relationship between it and its surroundings. It was therefore decided that the study area should include those parts of the landscape over which management control is immediately possible. Planting beyond this area is also to be considered.

A full variety of plant and animal life is part of our natural heritage. The object of this report is to suggest ways in which the present diversity may be enhanced. This can be achieved most easily by vegetation management, a rich flora invites and supports animals; the emphasis of the study is therefore on plants, it does not pretend to be a survey.

Existing habitats may be managed to increase their range, disturbance inherent in the design proposals can be minimised, and the design, where possible or desirable, may be detailed to hasten the naturally slow process of ecological succession to give the illusion of derivation from natural forces. Opportunities are apparent, in the lake design with varying depths, bank profiles and planting, in the planting of new woodlands with native species dominating, in the management of the grassland with the introduction of new species and in the wider planting of screen belts, copses, hedgerows and shrubs. Another aspect of diversity is more horticultural; there is space and opportunity to plant more exotic types of tree and shrub in areas about the house and parts of the wild garden. A collection of plants, rarer in cultivation, would add visual interest and variety and at the same time form a reservoir of these species.

The study area has been divided largely according to vegetation types, each smaller area is then dealt with in turn. The existing vegetation as seen during the study period, January - April unless otherwise stated, is described, its advantages and disadvantages in ecological and visual terms are appraised then, where appropriate, the implications of the design proposals are noted. In each case suggestions for new planting and different management techniques have been made. The division is arbitrary and only for the convenience of description. In nature there is a gradual transition from one vegetation zone to another and animals know few boundaries. The landscape should be regarded as a whole, its quality will be a reflection of man's capacity to manage changes which are the essence of nature. In ecological conservation, we look for a creative amalgam between preservation and control.

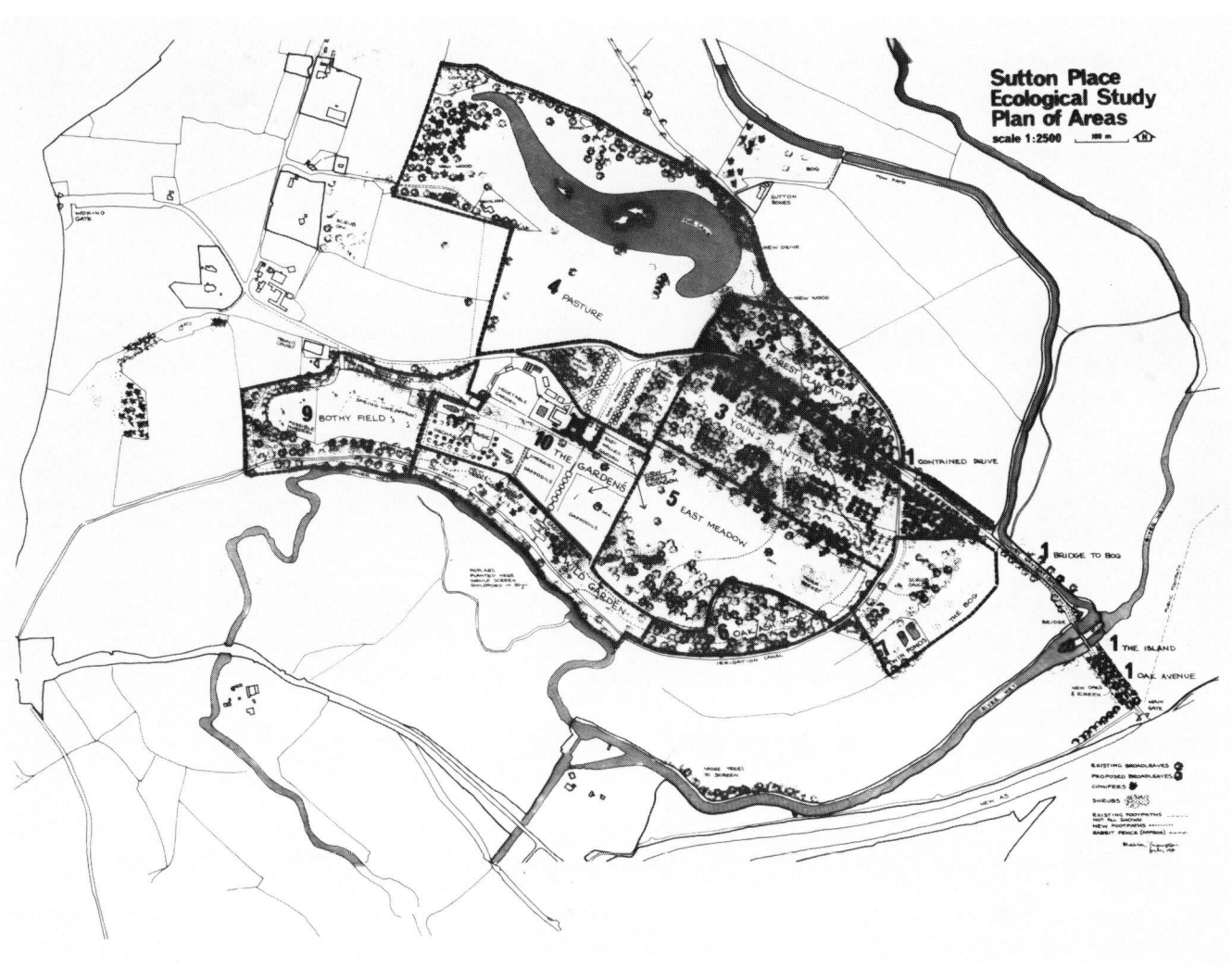

This study of the integration of ecological with architectural form was presented in ten parts.
The most influential modifications on the original concept were: 4 – the lake (page 160) and 8 – the
cascade (page 166).

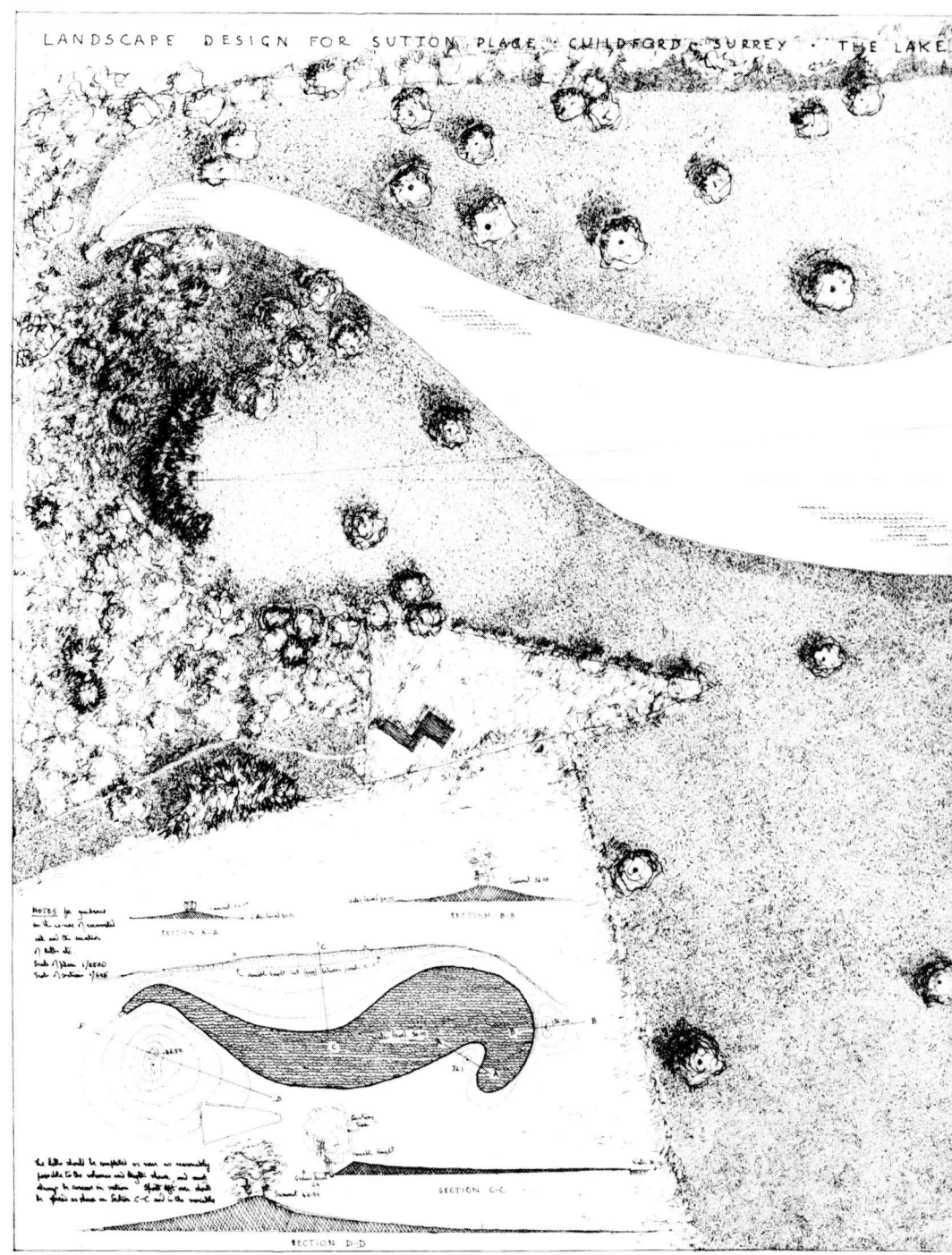

The lake

The lake was not included in the preliminary concept since the land form was such that no water at river level would be visible from the house. A few miles west at Painshill, however, Charles Hamilton in the eighteenth century had raised the waters of the River Wey several feet to form a lake of somewhat similar size. A raised twentieth century lake under the same circumstances and with modern mechanical equipment did not seem impossible and accordingly is now being made. The pure form of the concept did not allow for wild life of all kinds and the design has subsequently been enriched with three islands and sanctuaries along the coast.

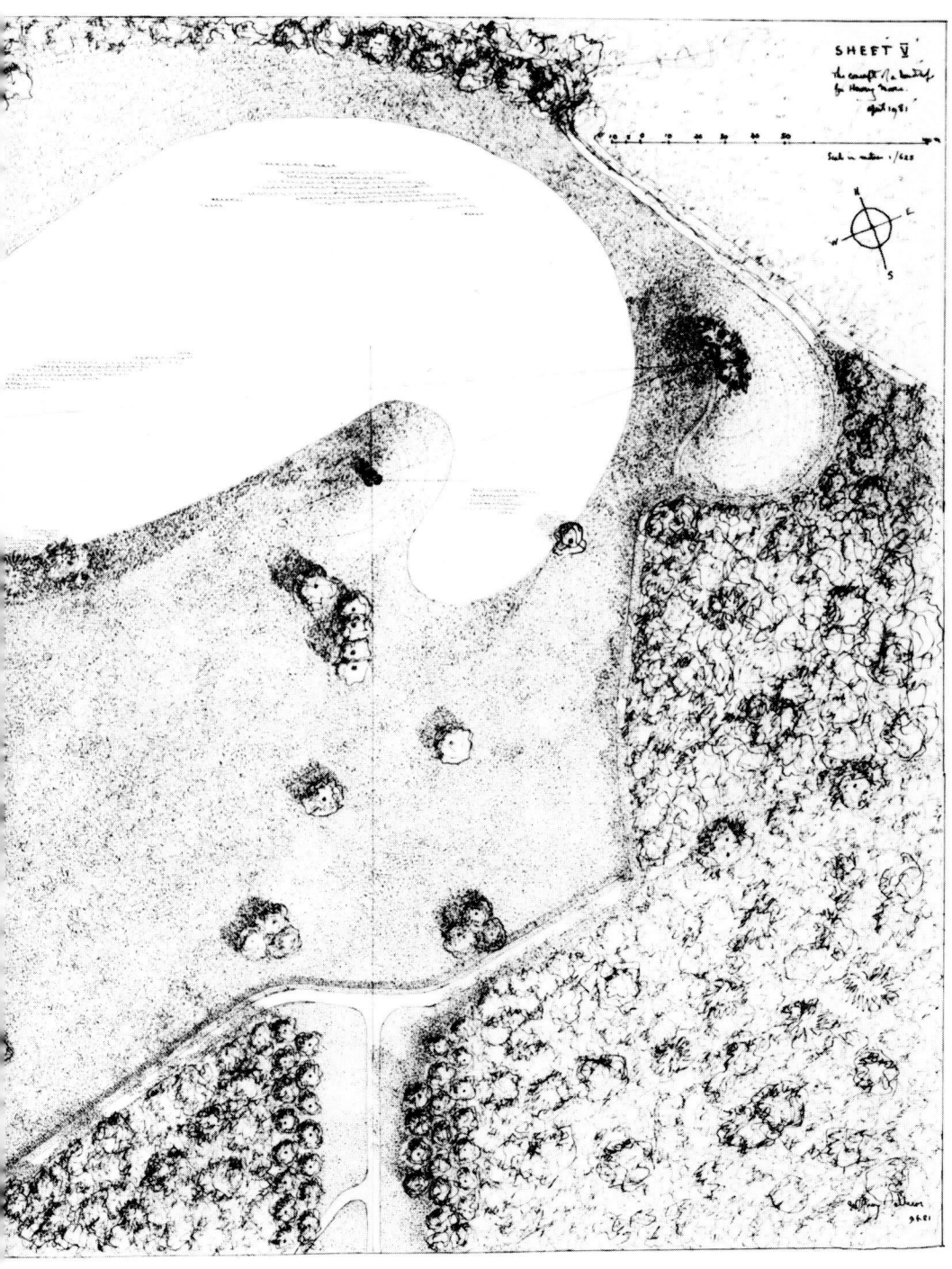

The lake is the beginning of the allegory. From its primeval depths had
emerged two natural hills: that to the west is the father figure, that to the east
is maternal. Between them and particularly under the eye of the mother
figure, will be an abstract sculpture, "Divided Oval", by Henry Moore, now
being cast in Hamburg (1983), the largest Moore sculpture in the world.
From these beginnings emerged all that is meant by civilisation.

It is proposed, with the sculptor's approval, to magnify this Carrara marble form eight times, in bronze. The sculptor has already approved the modelling around the lake in which it is to be set.

"Divided Oval", by Henry Moore (Stanley Seeger collection).

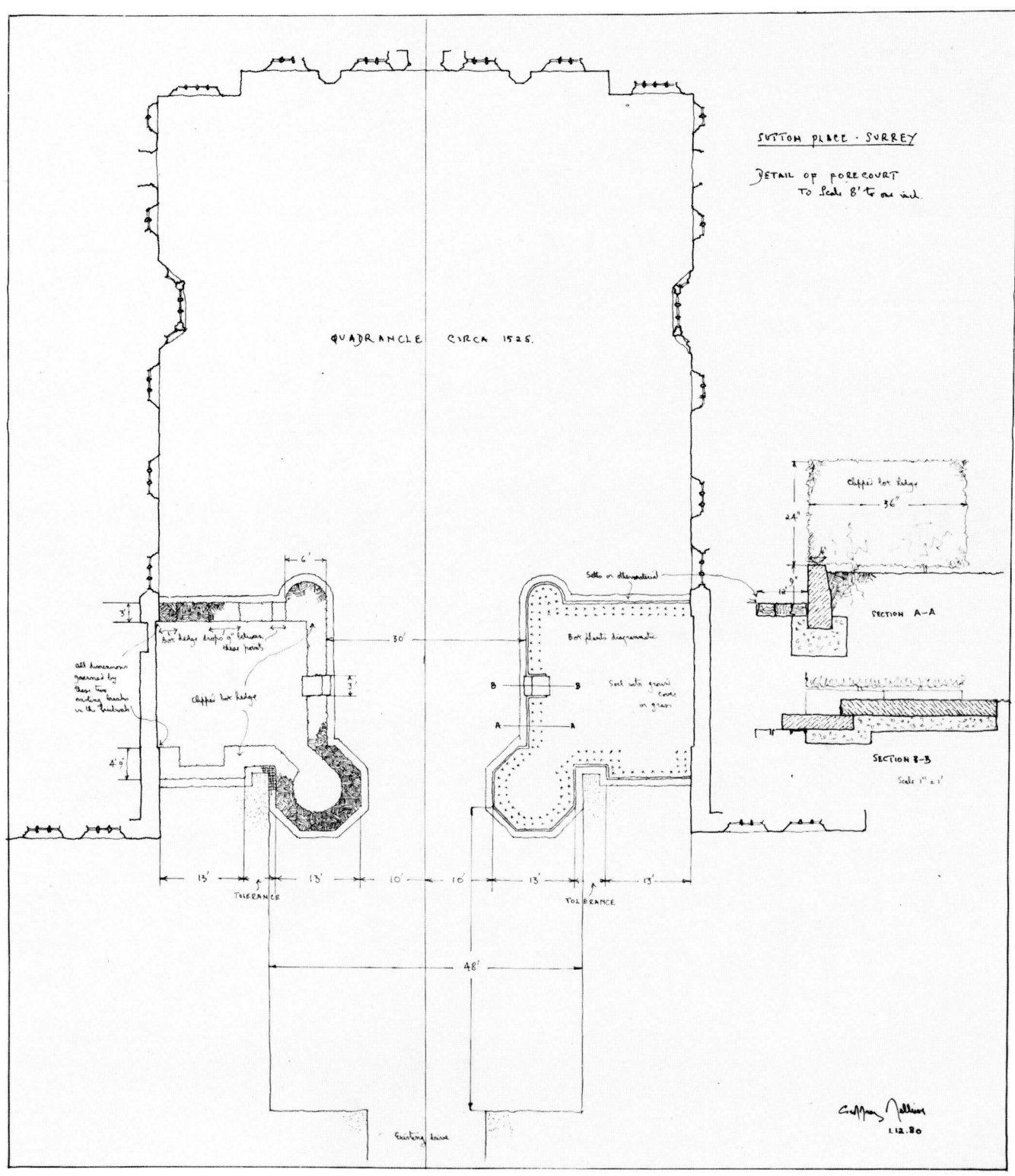

The forecourt.

To restore the proportions of the forecourt, a square, the plan of the original gatehouse has been outlined in clipped box hedge, set in a terracotta frame.

The landscape design is a continuation of historical phases I and II. It is possible to think of the gardens in 1980 in terms of a model, and over this a further model is to be placed, fitted in such a way that no part of the lower model were damaged.

The areas, from east to west, are as follows:

a) The east walled garden, balancing the existing west walled gardens. Divided into two by an existing yew hedge, this informal garden is in two parts, echoing Francis Bacon's description of the civilised adjoining the wild. The sculpture garden later became the secretive moss garden.

b) The long south walk leading from the east pavilion (later an octagon) through pleached limes that emphasise the basic classical symmetry, to a surrealistic terminus (later the Magritte garden).

c) The avenue of fountains, Persephone fountain, the grotto and the great cascade, modified later to retain all existing forest trees.

d) The Music theatre, remaining undetermined on grounds of external noise interference. Later a green theatre.

e) The walled swimming pool.

f) The walled kitchen garden.

g) The sculptured wall by Ben Nicholson, sited and made in close association with the artist. Note the change during the making of this drawing from one water design to another, both of which dissatisfied the artist and has been left as existing (at his special request). Nicholson did not live to see the completion of this great "project for a wall". The scale, like that of the lake, is heroic as befits the end of the allegory.

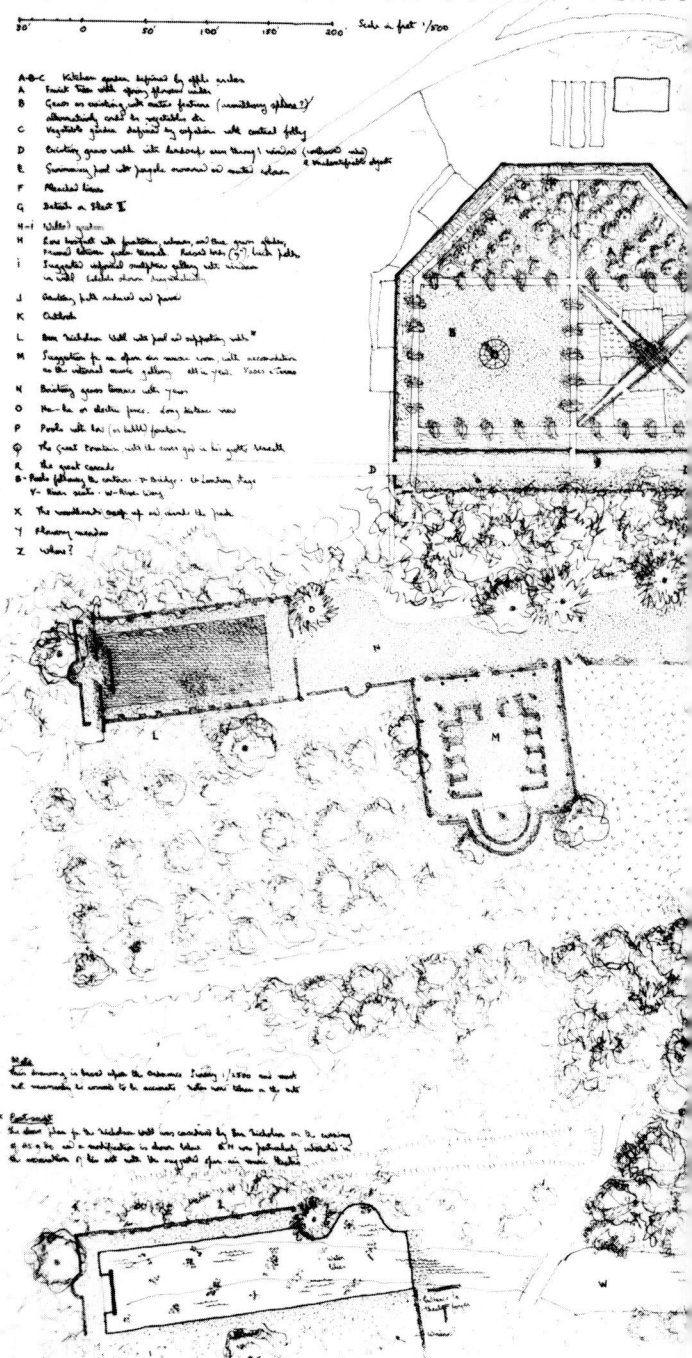

The areas round the house.
Plan made September 1980.

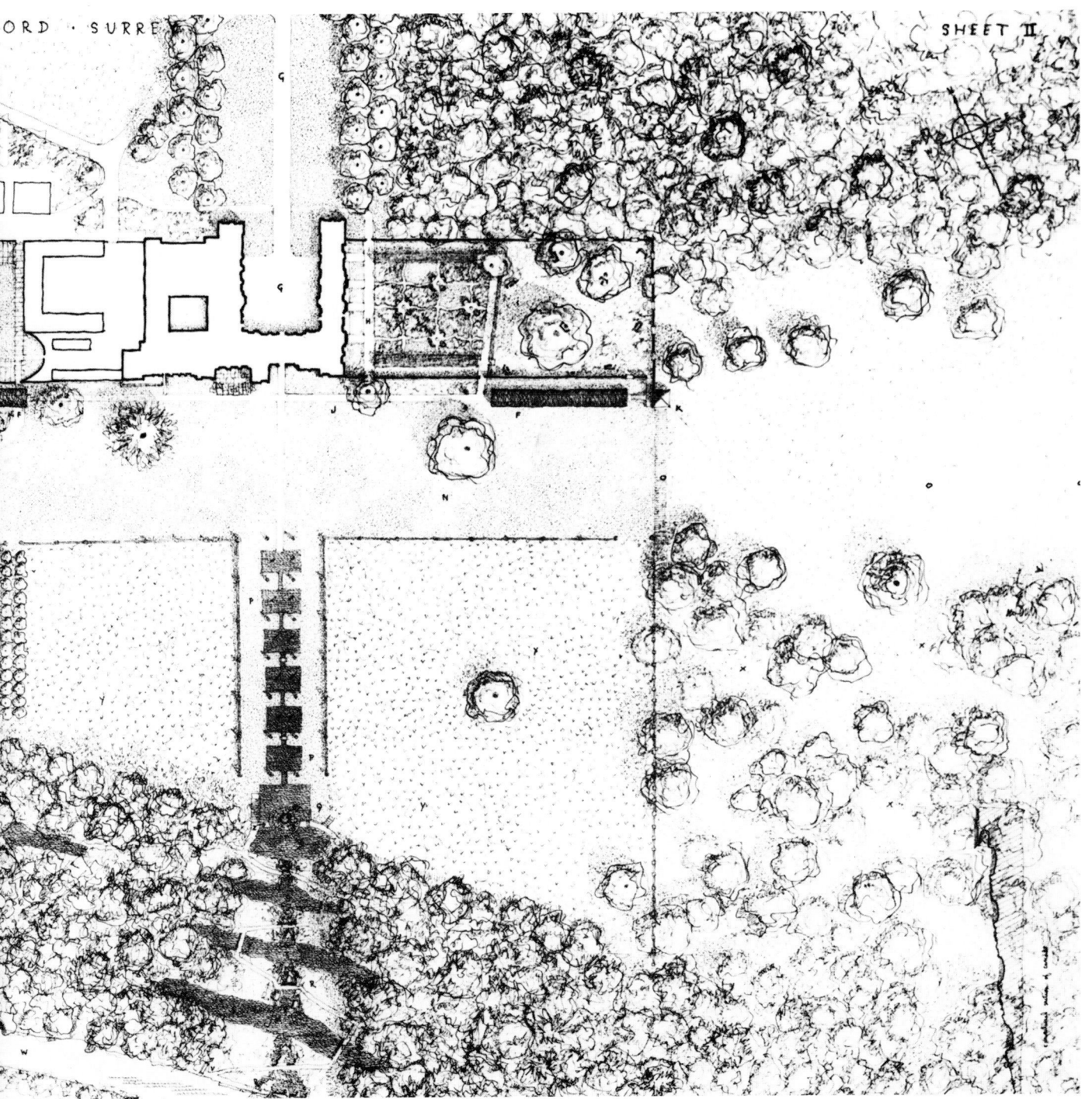

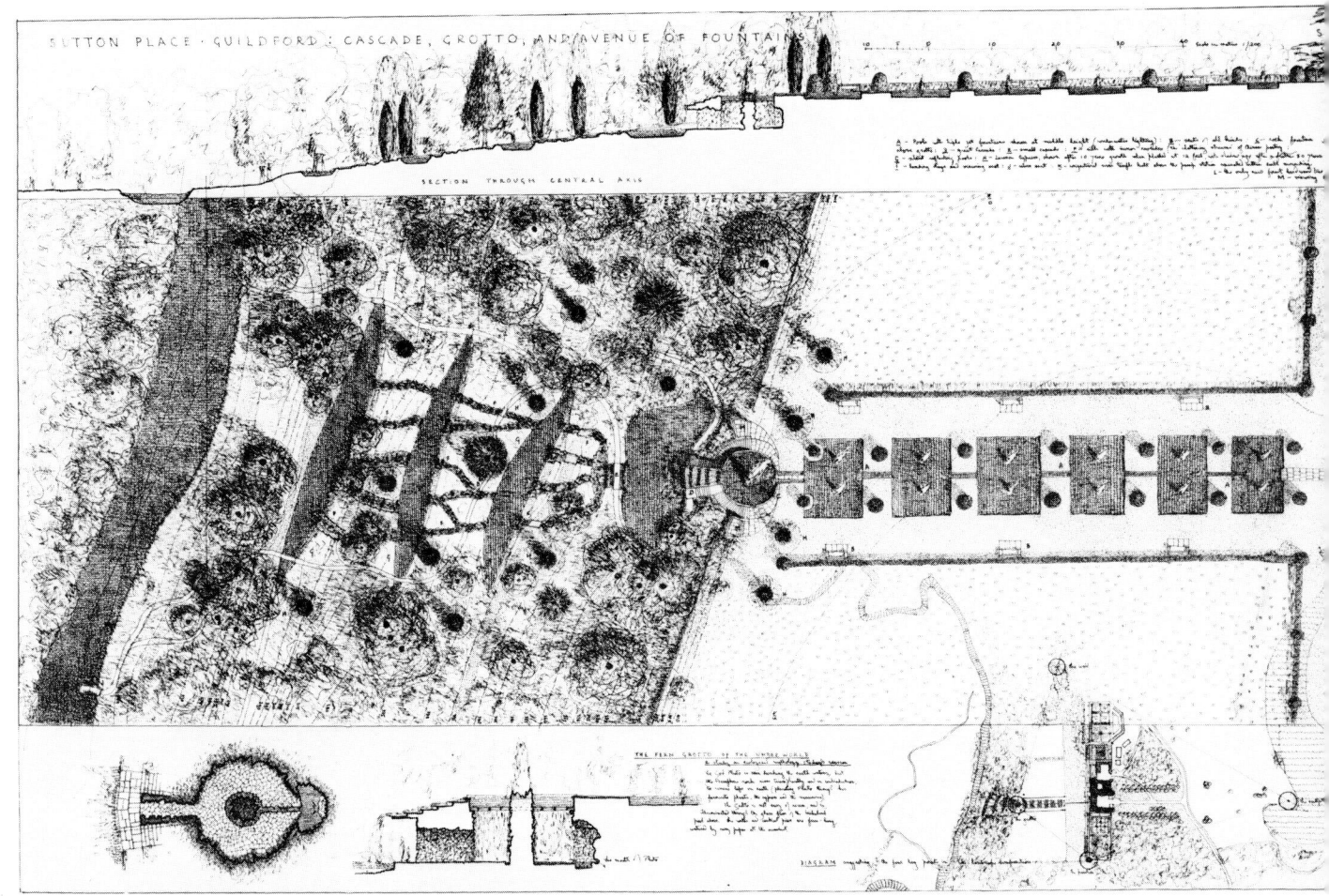

The avenue of fountains is interwoven with the existing clipped yews that continue the axiality of the historic composition. They lead to the Persephone fountain, whose source lies underground beneath the waters. To reach the grotto you must pass under the waterfall and thence along a dank dark passage. In the centre of the fern clad circle, illuminated through the water above, is the Persephone rock. Beyond is a sinister inner grotto, where the giant head of Pluto sucks in water . . . .

The form of the cascade is a change from that in the original concept, where it derived from Italianesque geometry. The practical factor of impeding the view from the house of distant industrial Guildford, combined with the ecological nature of the whole estate, caused the powerful baroque form to give way before the existing trees on their steep embankment. The water breaks into four chattering rills.

Avenue of Fountains,
Grotto and Cascade.
The works have
not yet begun.

Model for The Cascade.

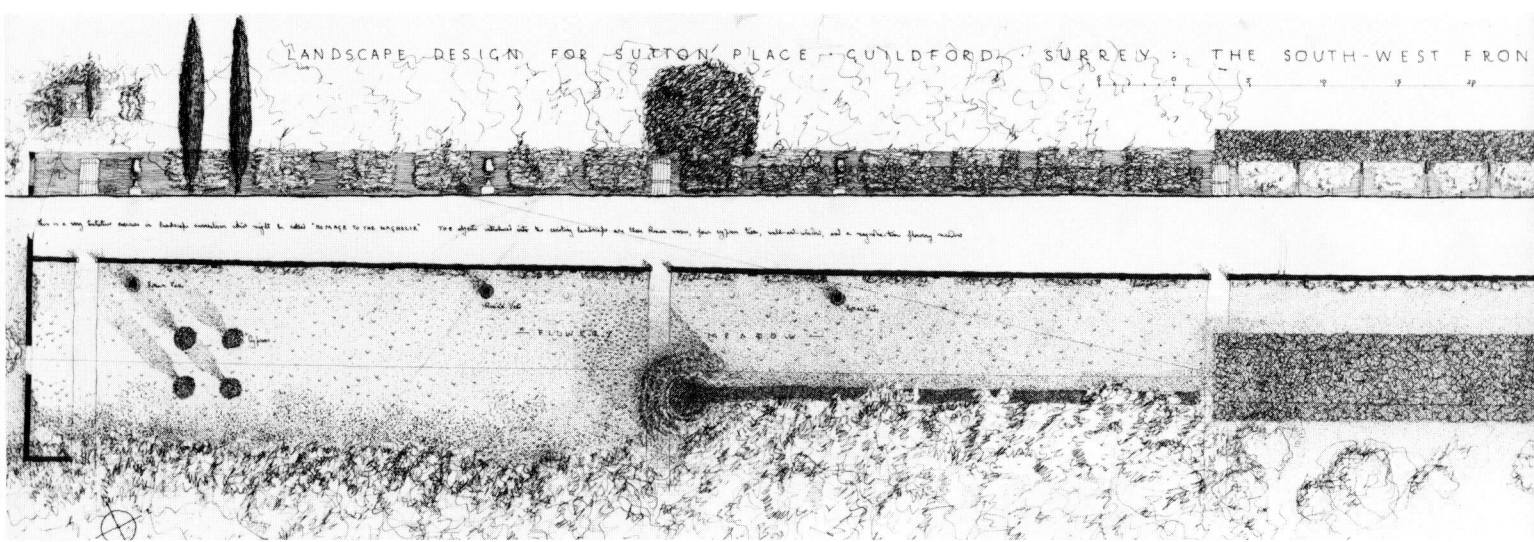

The south walk, looking east from the Magritte window.

The surrealistic landscape "Homage to the Magnolia" was inspired by the painter Magritte. The magnolia, being too small and tender itself to terminate such a lengthy vista, was framed and heralded by three (later five) monster Roman vases acquired from Mentmore. The purpose is to disorganise the mind by a deliberate incongruity in the juxtaposition of disparate objects, preparing it for the tranquility of the Nicholson wall.

The south walk passing the house eastwards towards the pavilion.

The south walk: passing the east walled garden.

The gardens are balanced about the house in time as well as space. The house represents a past whose humanistic values will prevail and whose authority over all is reinforced by the architectural pleached limes. The gardens to the west are surrealist, those to the east are of the present or near-present.

The long walk terminates on the east in a pavilion (now an octagon) whose domed and painted interior looks out upon the four pleasurable elements in the landscape that have fashioned civilised man. The window towards the moss garden overlooks the landscape of dreams and imagination; the second window sees the forest from which as *Homo erectus* he emerged with all faculties complete; the third window looks upon the savannah country in which he hunted for survival and which inspired the English eighteenth century school of landscape; and the fourth upon the work of the settler and classical man.

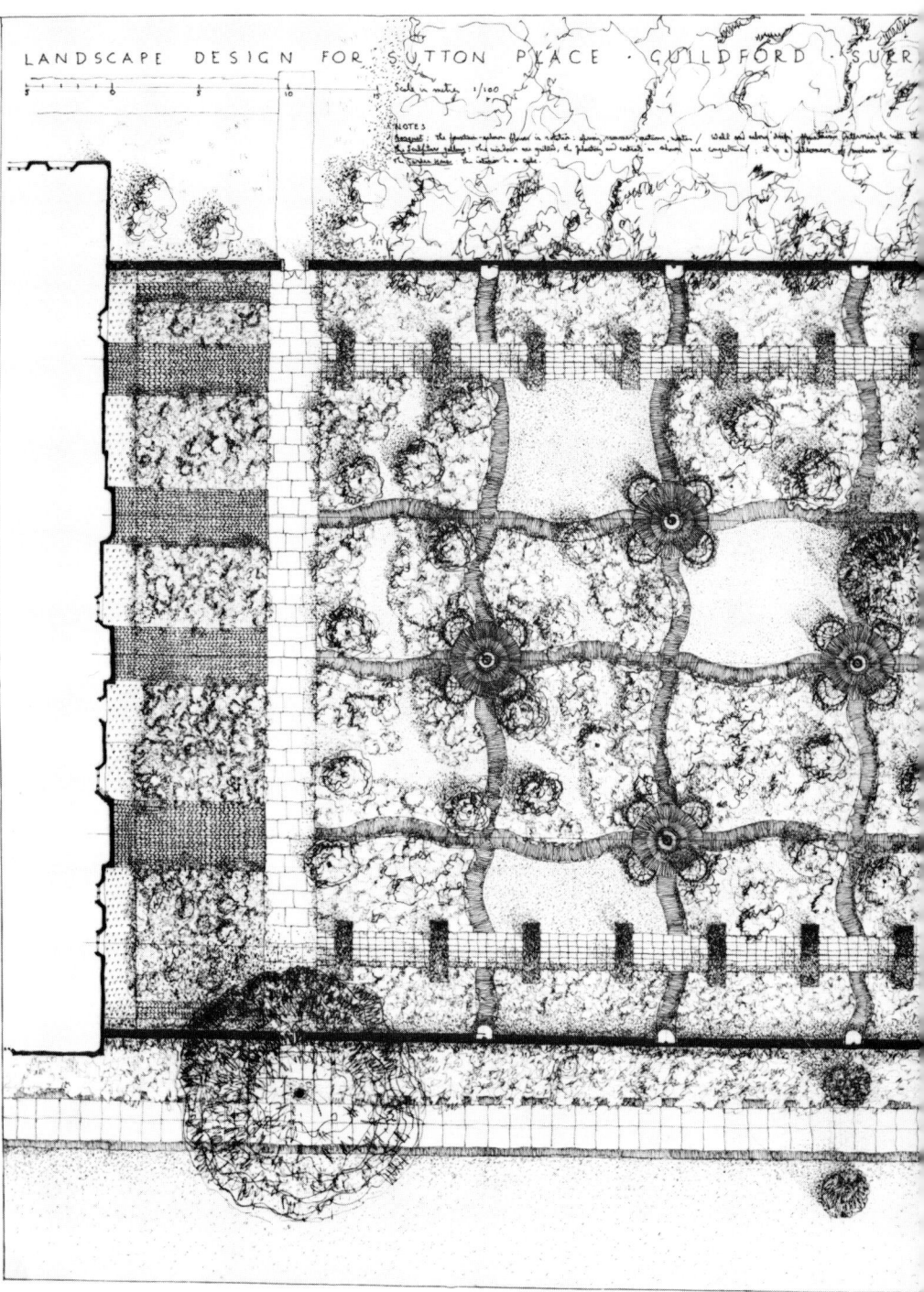

East walled garden: plan
dated December 1980.

Since this drawing was made the enclosure has been divided into three rather
than two parts, as follows:

a) The space between house and cross path, dominated by the chimney
breasts, is now a moat overlooked by lily observation balconies and crossed by
stepping stones. The allegory is that you must have a hazardous journey if you
are to reach . . . .

b) The paradise garden on the further side of the moat. This is a pleasure
garden rich with flowers, arbours and fountains for the sensual enjoyment of

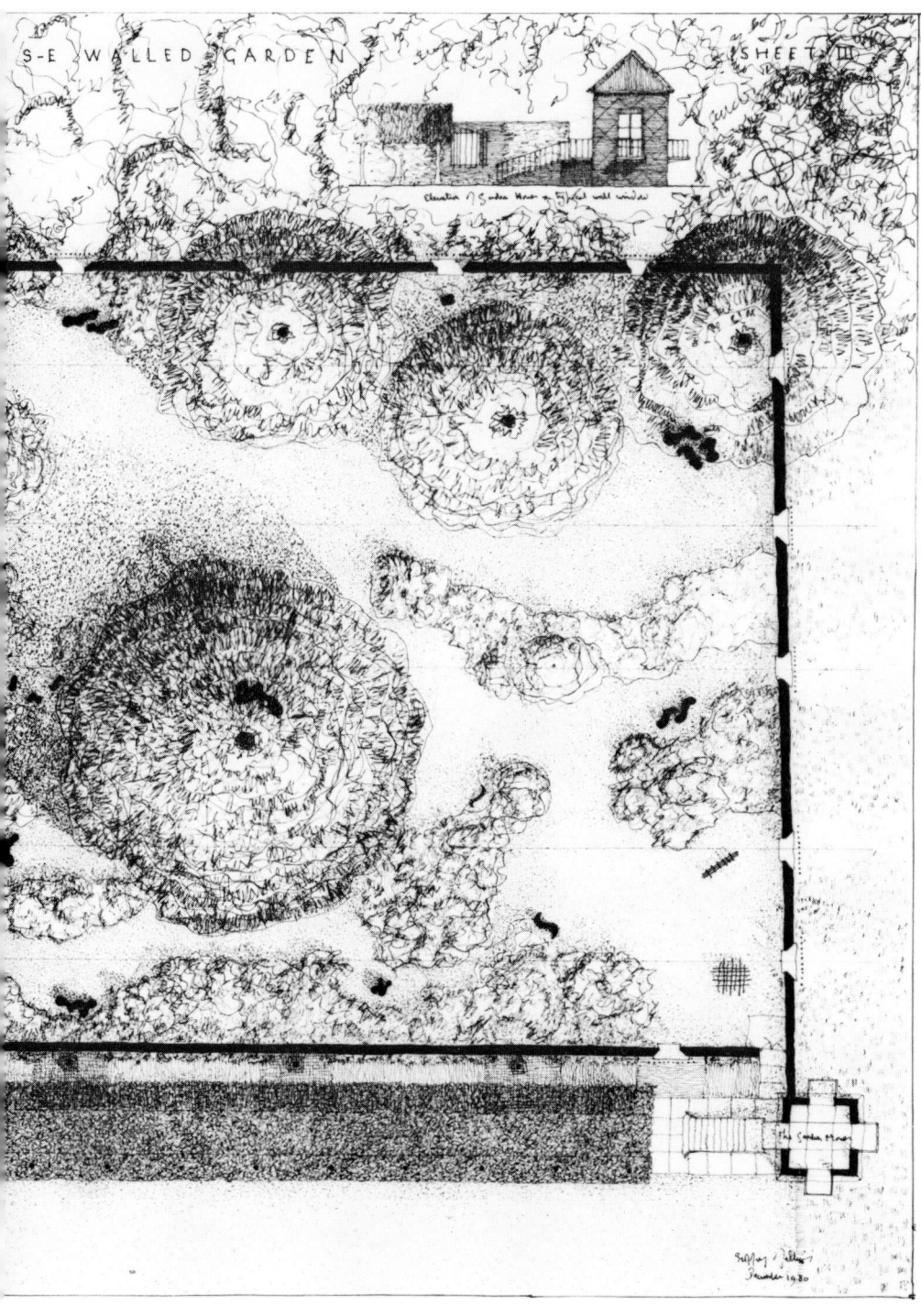

the moment. The paths took their earth-worm shapes from the curlings of the Tudor chimneys. The arbours are for conversation, the grass glades for contemplation and the pleasaunce generally for music of water, bees and birds. Beyond the pleasaunce is the . . .

c) Wild garden with its one great plane and two smaller. Designed in this plan as a green exhibition gallery for modern sculpture, it subsequently changed into the moss or secret garden (page 180).

Irises by Claude Monet (Stanley Seeger collection).

The artist is necessarily in advance of the landscape designer in feeling new relationships with the environment. In the house are modern works of art, abstract and/or figurative, which have a direct bearing on landscape design. One of the pioneers into this world beyond the senses was Monet, whose gardens at Giverny sought to anchor on earth the conception of the inconstancy and flux in which we are enmeshed. The argument is that just as the artist releases certain frustrations from the subconscious of the spectator, so could the landscape designer – and perhaps even more so since the spectator himself is a participator.

The lily pool, east walled garden.

The water balconies are observation points for lilies and fish, as well as the far-off paradise gardens. Contrary to the accepted view of a moat, the pool itself is defensive against too easy an access from the house. The allegory calls for stepping stones as an approach to paradise, so hazardous that only the brave will attempt the crossing.

The Paradise Garden: arches leading from the house to the moss or secret garden.

The Paradise Garden: the conversation arbours grouped round the bird-bath fountains. The sound of water, enriched by the deeper tones of six spouting wall fountains, is intended to be a background only to the speaking voice. Elsewhere, there is stillness. The plants climbing up each of the four groups flower at different times throughout the summer.

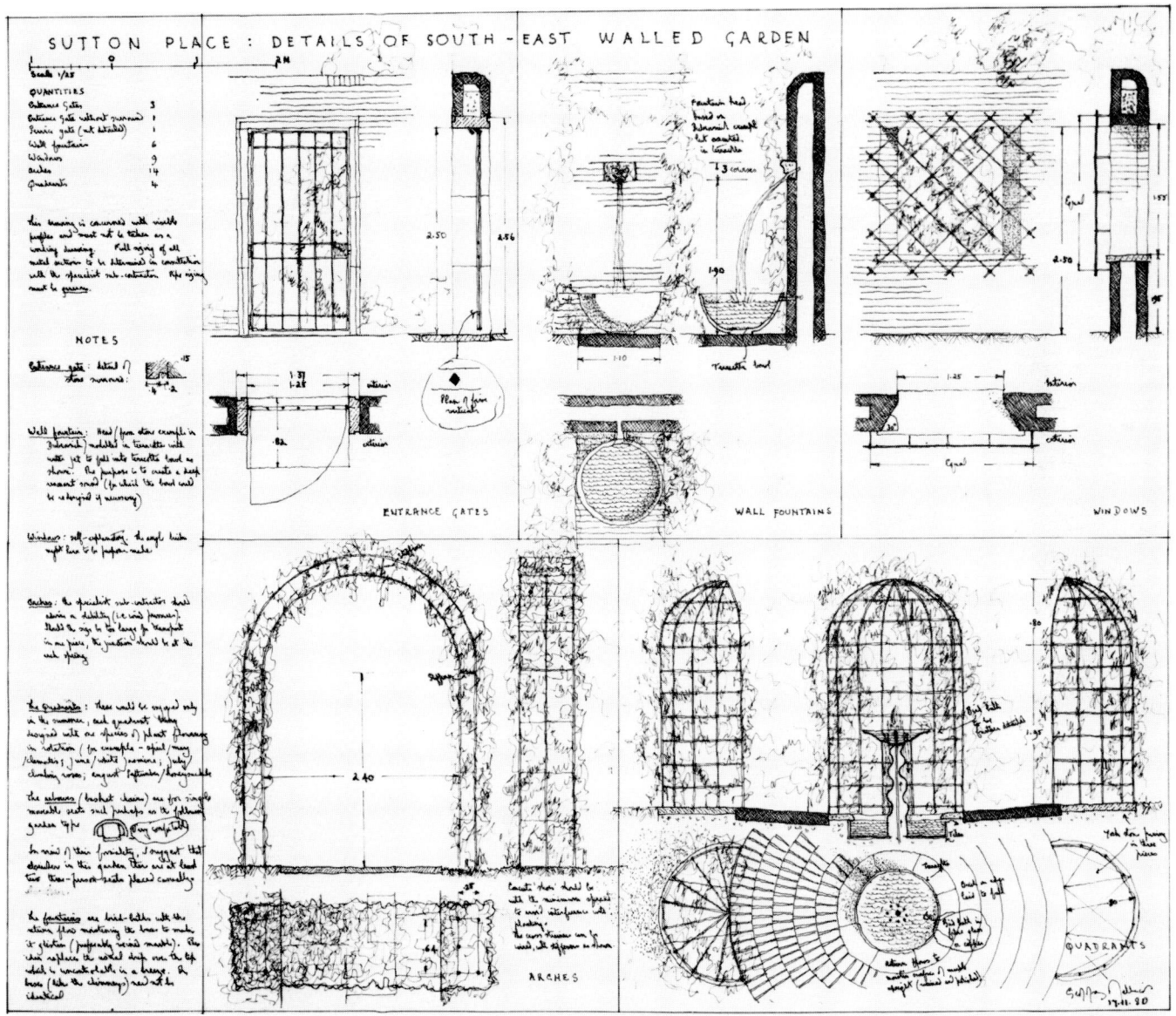

The east walled garden: Details.

To copy the historic form of the past is to raise a corpse from the dead and pretend it is alive. Only the spirit can be alive to activate the present. It is intended that all detail should be a study of pure form influenced by but not echoing the old. Whereas the dress, as it were, is twentieth century placed beside the sixteenth century, the body within, with its instincts for commodity, firmness and delight is much the same.

Looking into the moss garden.

Looking outwards from the moss garden.

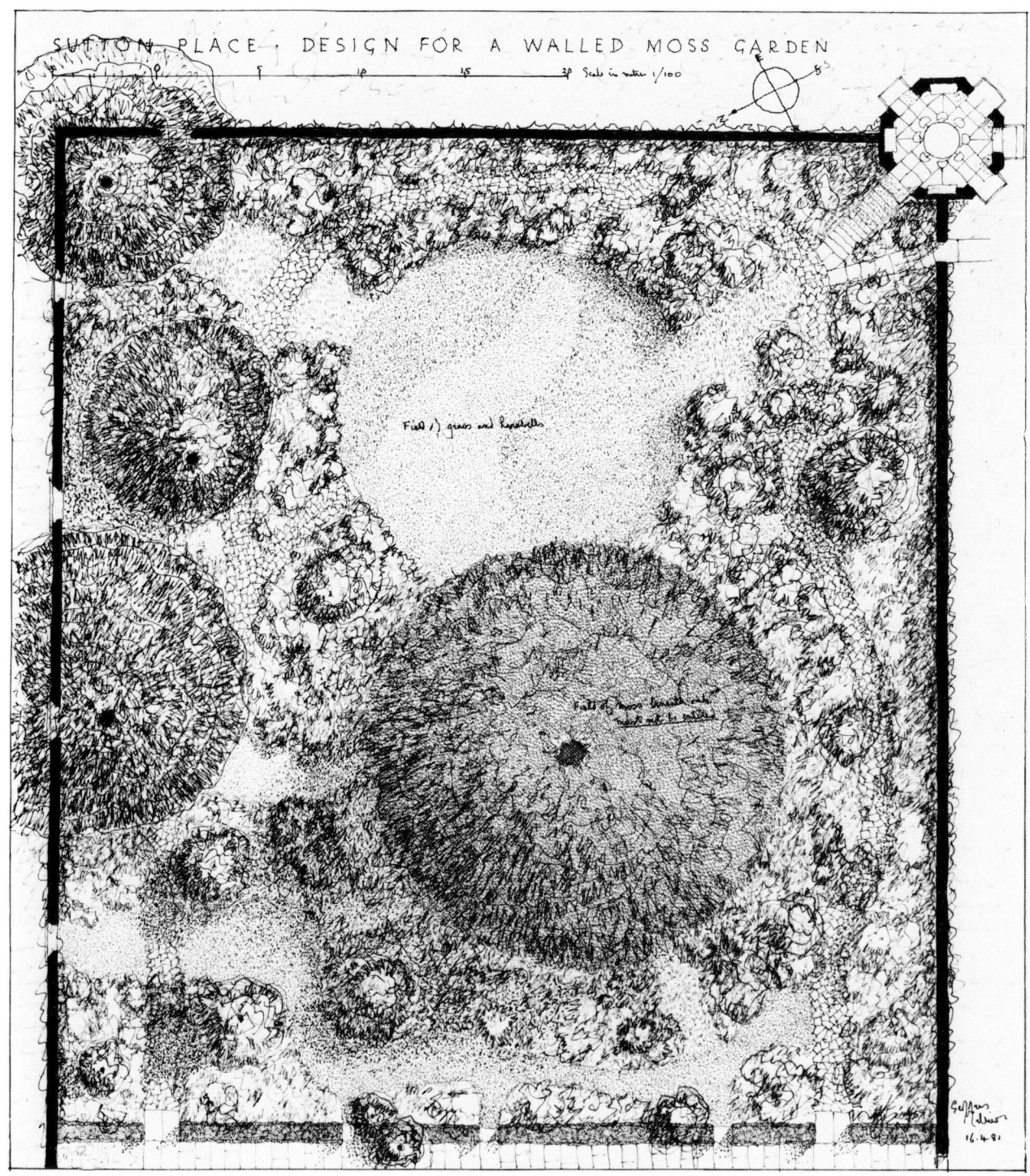

The moss garden.

The moss or secret garden lies beyond the paradise garden and is the heart of the grand allegory. Within us lurk associations of the ideas of childhood, some of which indeed are a sub-conscious, pre-natal inheritance. The child's imagination is not confined to what it sees, for it creates pictures beyond the power of the adult educated in the rational.

The two interlocking circles hidden in the centre can be interpreted as each of us pleases, with this proviso only: that you can enter the grass circle, but not the moss under the plane tree.

Midsummer Night 1876 by
Atkinson Grimshaw
(Stanley Seeger Collection).

The terms of reference of the garden to take the place of the sculpture garden
as proposed, were the interpretation of this picture together with the inclusion
of all plants described in an early book on flowers. The search for what lay
behind this request involved a deep psychological study that paradoxically
seems to have been unconsciously influenced by the Nicholson wall. The
findings were that there are certain undisclosed yearnings that remain
throughout life common to all.

Sutton Place

Moss garden: planting plan.
Three stages in the realisation of the moss garden (and planting elsewhere) are: 1) the original conception on page 180 which conveys the spirit of intention, 2) the interpretation of the planting into reality by Susan Jellicoe, and 3) the transcription of this into a precise planting plan by Hilary Shrive, who also superintended the execution. It may be ten years before the garden attains the mystery suggested in the original drawing.

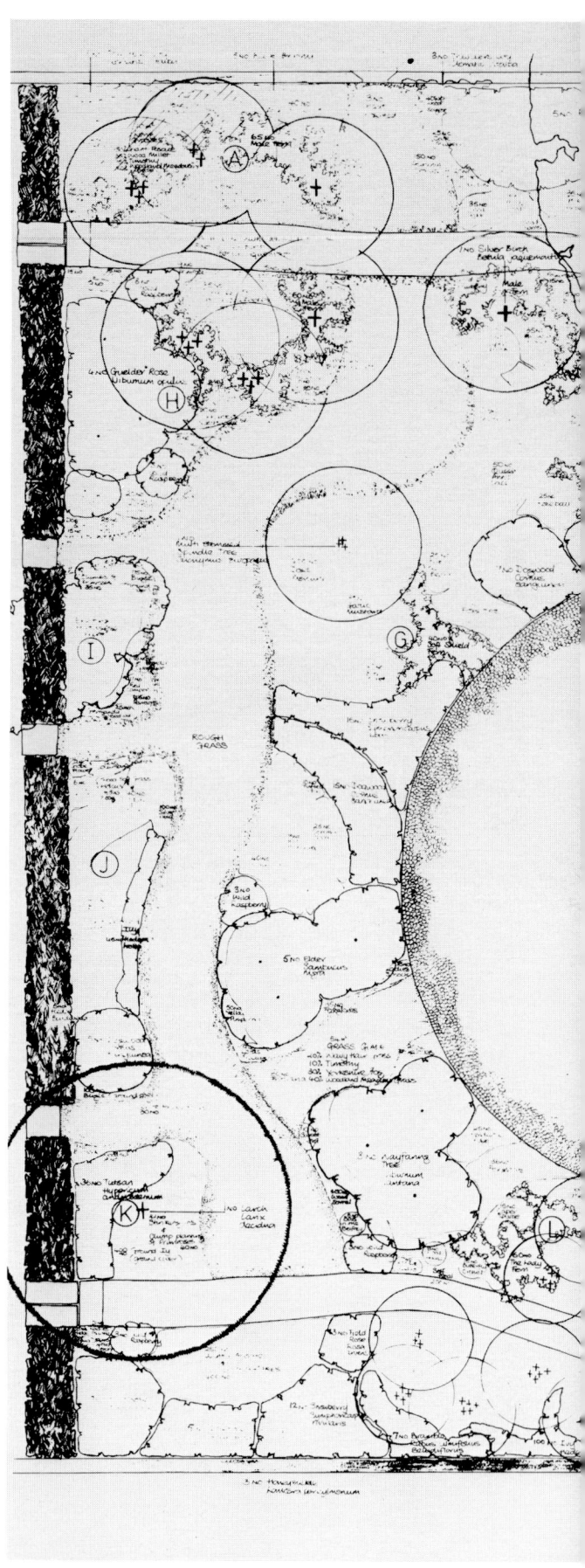

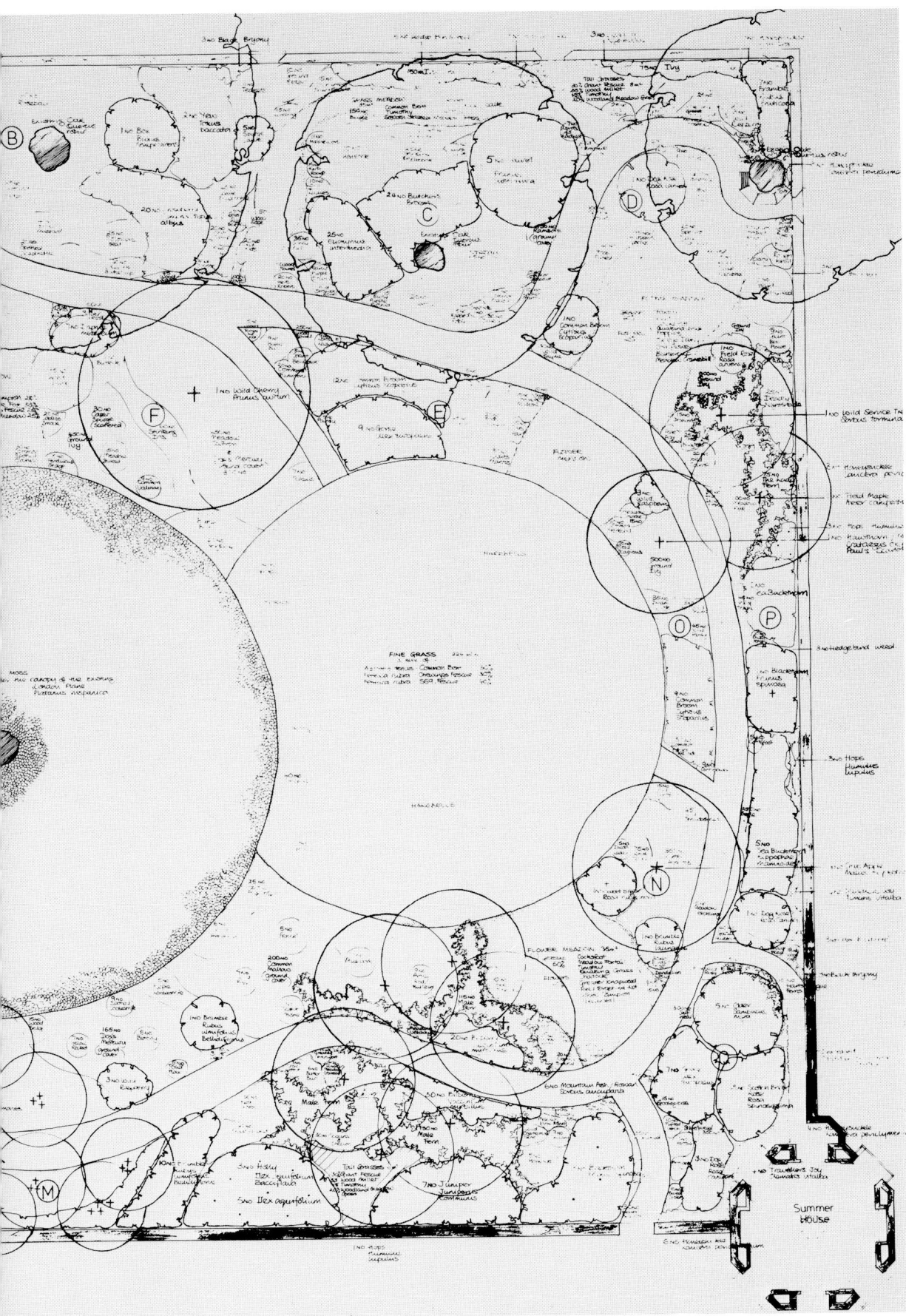

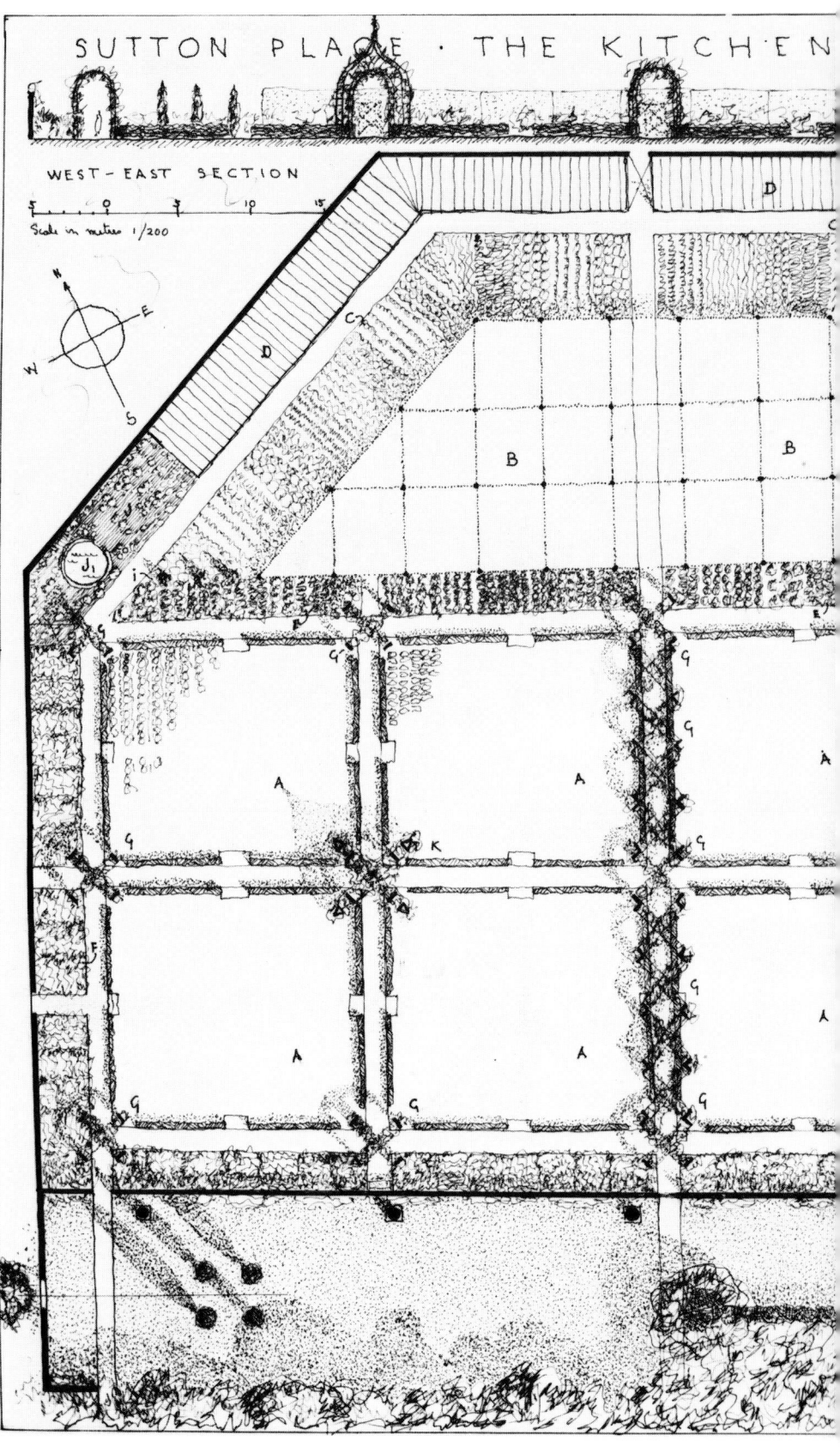

West walled and
Magritte gardens.

Although the swimming pool, kitchen garden and surrealist garden cannot be
seen together visually, they present in combination that mix of the rational

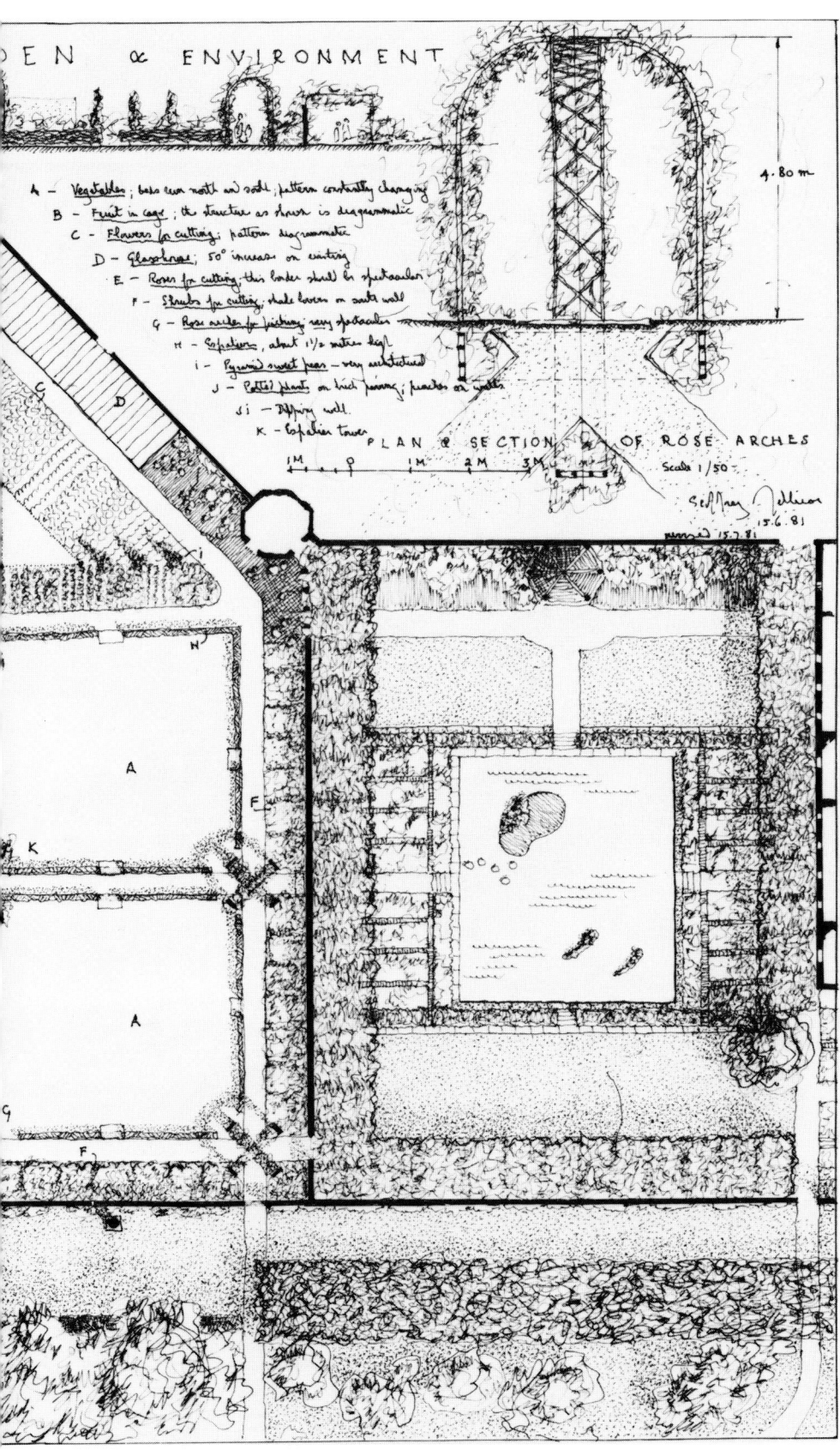

A — Vegetables; beds run north and south, pattern constantly changing

B — Fruit in cage; the structure as shown is diagrammatic

C — Flowers for cutting; pattern diagrammatic

D — Glasshouse; 50° increase on exterior

E — Roses for cutting; this border shall be spectacular

F — Shrubs for cutting; shale lovers on south wall

G — Rose arches for picking; very spectacular

H — Espaliers, about 1½ metres high

I — Pyramid sweet peas — very architectural

J — Potted plants on brick paving; peaches on walls

Ji — Dipping well

K — Espalier tower

PLAN & SECTION OF ROSE ARCHES

Scale 1/50

4.80 m

Geoffrey Jellicoe

15.6.81

and irrational, of the sensible and incomprehensible, that is the chief delight of garden design.

185

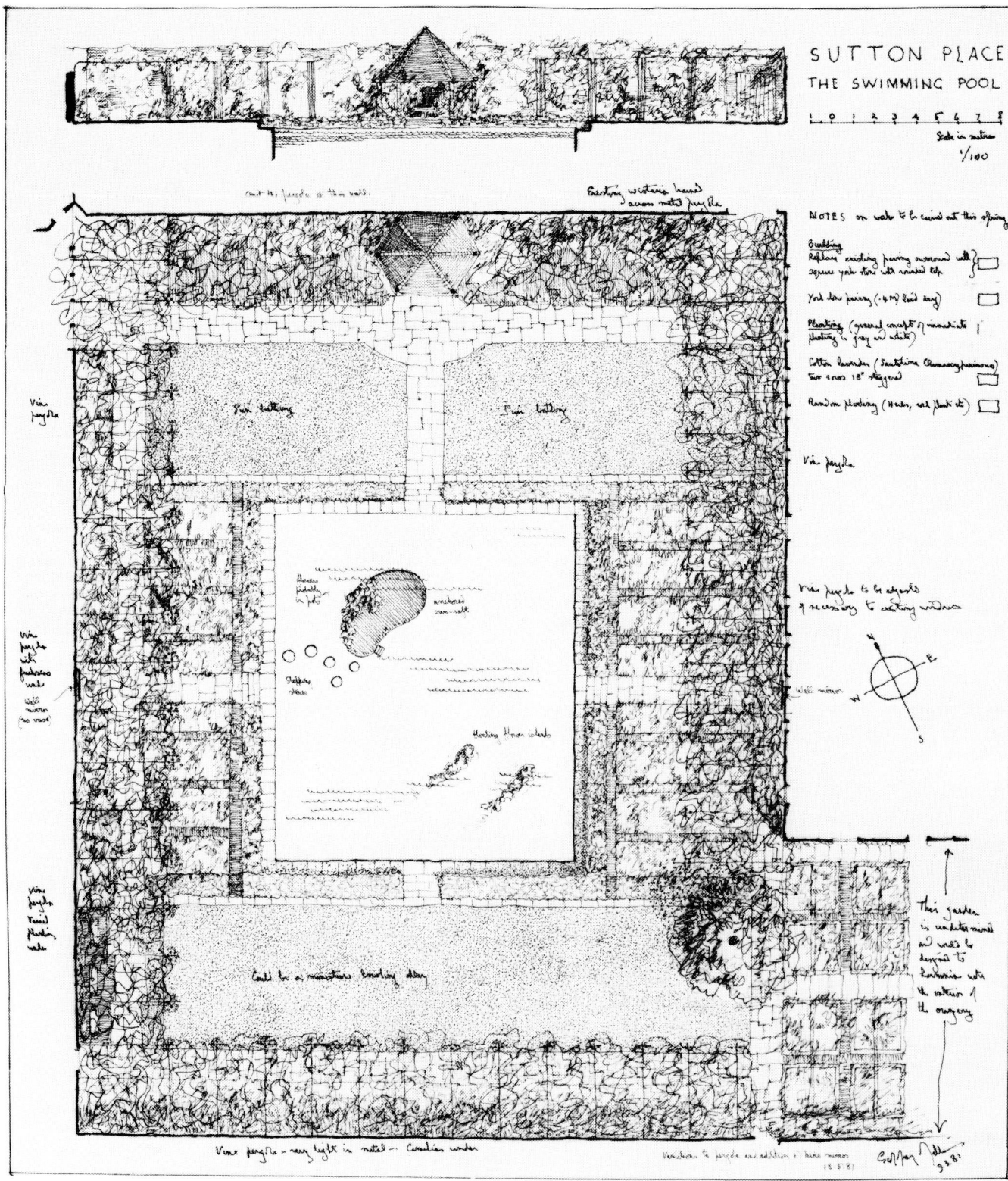

The swimming pool.

The pool is surrounded by a covered vine walk, recalling (to the art historian) the cool garden arcades that Weston must have seen in the Touraine. On the light reflecting surface of the water are stepping stones to an anchored and flowered sun raft. Two smaller rafts float by promiscuously. The water picture was originally inspired by Miró and is known as "The Miró Mirror".

186

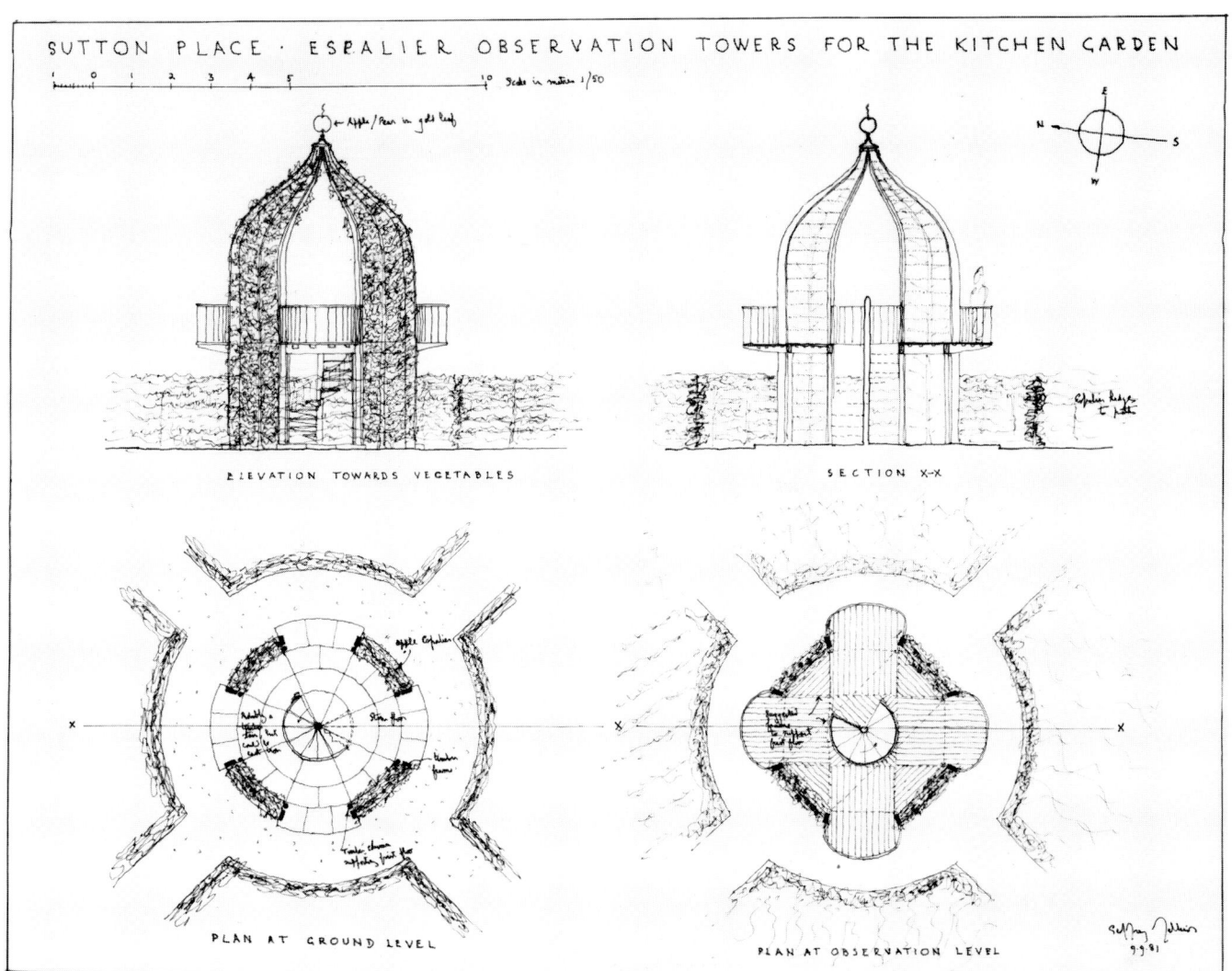

ELEVATION TOWARDS VEGETABLES

SECTION X-X

PLAN AT GROUND LEVEL

PLAN AT OBSERVATION LEVEL

The two main squares of the kitchen gardens are defined by apple and pear espaliers. Within each square is a further subdivision into four squares. Within all eight of these subsidiary squares lie everchanging patterns of vegetables. To look down upon this restless continuum are two observation towers, known as "Espalier Escalier towers" and crowned respectively with a gold apple and pear.

187

Today, a table and chair sit upon the sun raft in the swimming pool garden, and apples are being planted in the kitchen garden next to it.

The Beautiful Truths (1964), by René Magritte.

The Magritte garden entitled "Homage to the Magnolia" seen through the window. On the left the green tunnel leading to the Nicholson Wall.

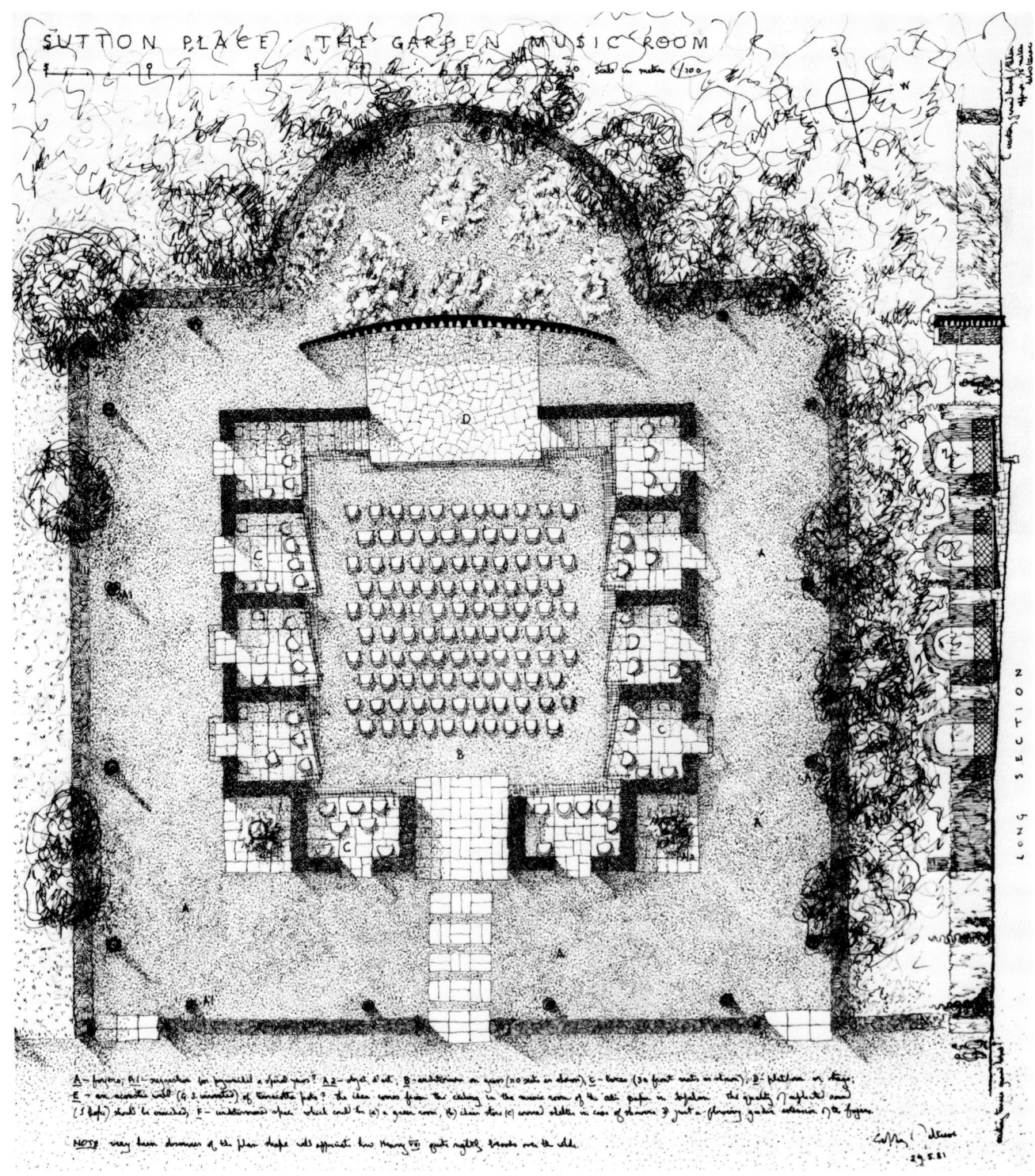

The Garden Music Room.

Due to the unpredictable English weather the theatre was designed to accommodate the same number of audience as could be fitted into the long gallery. Even in Italy, where it originated, the garden theatre was regarded first as an ornament and folly, setting fire to the imagination even when empty. The drawing carries with it the following enigmatic note: "Very keen observers of the land shape will appreciate how Henry VIII broods over the whole". The king was himself a composer.

190

Model with later variations.

The concept plan suggested that the music room could be more than a folly, but in order to make it viable as a practical theatre, hard paths would be needed at least to serve the boxes, together with bar, lavatories and chair store.

The stage being too unfriendly for a quartet, a tree with spreading branches was to be moved into the centre. The acoustic wall would be made of terracotta resonant pots in various sizes. In the event acoustic experts found that the sound of distant traffic on a still evening would be disturbing, and execution has been deferred. Now re-designed as an open-air green theatre. Model by June Harrison.

Since he evolved his abstract reliefs in the early thirties it had been the artist's ambition to transfer a "project for a wall" into outdoor reality. Except a temporary "Relief Wall" in Documenta III exhibition 1964 at Kassel, and despite at least six attempts in this country, no Nicholson wall previous to that at Sutton Place has been erected. Indestructible, in specially chosen Carrara marble (the great circle was carved from a single stone), it measures thirty-two feet by sixteen feet, approximately.

The original, selected jointly by Stanley Seeger and Ben Nicholson, is in the Albright Knox Art Gallery, Buffalo and is entitled *White Relief 1937/38*. It is oil on carved mahogany and measures 126 × 64 cm.

The artist did not live to see the finished wall, nor the moss garden, which it had informed.

White Relief 1937/38
by Ben Nicholson. Model.
The setting dates from 1905.

Nicholson wall seen middle distance. The idea of weightlessness derived from the Kennedy Memorial (pages 98-99).

The artist who seems most to have influenced Ben Nicholson was Mondrian. This artist, like Plato before him, conceived the essence of all form to be mathematical, illustrating his point (for example) through a series of sketches of a tree that he reduced, and finally blasted, into pure geometry. Nicholson also dedicated his life to the creation of pure form, but unlike Mondrian (who seems to have detested plant growth) he loved nature and its intricacies. More than any twentieth century artist he resolved the absolute balance, authority and grandeur of the laws of the universe into the beautiful untidiness of the natural laws of organic growth, which he did not pretend or wish to understand.

He insisted that the foreground to his exquisitely balanced composition should be of casual water-lilies. In later life, perhaps subconsciously influenced by the new space/time dimensions, he explored deeply into the mind, bringing up strange phantasies with meanings he could not explain.

Sutton Place

Of this design Ben Nicholson said: "You know, it is interesting that had the smaller circle been two inches higher, the design would have been without meaning." When asked what he meant by "meaning," he replied, "how should *I* know?"

Sir Geoffrey Jellicoe

Born London 8th October 1900. Educated
Cheltenham College and Architectural Association,
London. Married Susan Pares 1936. Past President,
Institute of Landscape Architects; member Royal
Institute of British Architects; member Royal Town
Planning Institute; member of Royal Fine Arts
Commission 1954-68; Trustee of the Tate Gallery
1966-73. Hon. President, International Federation
of Landscape Architects. 1981 medallist of the
American Society of Landscape Architects.
Publications include: *Italian Gardens of the Renaissance*
1925 (jointly with J.C. Shepherd); *Studies in Landscape
Design*, vols. I, II and III; *The Landscape of Man* 1975
(jointly with Susan Jellicoe). Apart from landscape,
the town planning and architectural practice included
Hemel Hempstead New Town and Plymouth Civic
Centre. Created Commander of the British Empire
1963. Knighted 1979 for services to landscape
architecture.

SOURCE OF ILLUSTRATIONS

INDEX

Production Credits and Materials:

Design:
David Bartholomew

Production Coordination:
Peter D. Taylor
Print Publication Services
Office for Educational Practice

Typesetting and Assembly:
Buchanan Graphics
London, Ontario

Indexing:
Chris Blackburn

Printing and Binding:
Johanns Graphics Limited
Waterloo, Ontario

Typestyle:
Baskerville

Paper Stock and Dust Jacket:
160M Warren's Patina, Matte Finish
200M Imperial Offset Enamel

Softcover:
12 point Kromekote Cover
130M Byronic Cover, Twilight Grey

Hardcover:
Millbank Linen